Tonga Proverbs
for Teaching and Preaching

This book is part of the African Proverbs Project, 1993-1997, with assistance from The Pew Charitable Trusts, Philadelphia, USA

This book was published in the Tonga language in 2000 (ISBN 99908-16-36-0) and may be ordered from Kachere Series, Box 1037, Zomba, Malawi.

Published by
Kachere Series
P.O. Box 1037, Zomba, Malawi
ISBN: 99908-76-10-X
Kachere Books no. 18

The Kachere Series is represented outside Africa by
African Books Collective, Oxford (www.africanbookscollective.com)
Michigan State University Press, East Lansing (www.msupress.msu.edu)

Layout: Mercy Chilunga and Gladys Phiri
Cover design: Mercy Chilunga
Illustrations: Isaiah Mphande

Printed by Lightning Source

TONGA PROVERBS
FOR TEACHING AND PREACHING

David K. Mphande

Kachere Books no. 18
Zomba
2006

Kachere Series
P.O. Box 1037, Zomba, Malawi
kachere@globemw.net
www.sndp.org.mw/kachereseries/

This book is part of the Kachere Series, a range of books on religion, culture and society from Malawi. Related Kachere books are:

Boston Soko, *Nchimi Chikanga: The Battle against Witchcraft in Malawi*

David Mphande, *Nthanthi za Chitonga*

Ian Dicks, *Wisdom of the Yao People*

John McCracken, *Politics and Christianity in Malawi 1875-1940*

Joseph Chakanza, *Wisdom of the People: 2000 Chinyanja Proverbs*

Margaret Sinclair, *Salt and Light. The Letters of Jack and Mamie Martin from Malawi*

Masiye Tembo, *Touched by His Grace: A Ngoni Story of Tragedy and Triumph*

Orison Ian Mkandawire, *Chiswakhata Mkandawire of Livingstonia*

Silas S. Ncozana, *The Spirit Dimension in African Christianity. A Pastoral Study among Tumbuka People of Northern Malawi*

Stephen Kauta Msiska, *Golden Buttons. Christianity and Traditional Religion among the Tumbuka*

The Kachere Series is the publications arm of the Department of Theology and Religious Studies of the University of Malawi.

Series Editors: J.C. Chakanza, F.L. Chingota, Klaus Fiedler, Chimwemwe Katumbi, P.A. Kalilombe, S. Mahommad, Martin Ott

Table of Contents

Foreword

The Proverbs for Preaching and Teaching Series is one facet of the many-sided African Proverbs Project (see Appendix B), an international, interdisciplinary effort to promote the collection, study and publication of proverbs. Proverbs are an endangered heritage of African peoples, under increasing heat from Western influences including Western education.

The Project was organized to find and encourage the people who are already working to preserve and promote African proverbs as well as to recruit additional people to blaze some new trails in proverb study and use. The Proverbs for Preaching and Teaching Series is one of these new trails, perhaps the most promising one. Rev. Joshua Kudadjie of Ghana, Rev. Abba Karnga of Liberia and Rev. David Mphande, all with long experience in preaching and religious education, were recruited to pioneer the way by producing annotated proverb collections in their own languages.

Many other African proverb collections have been written and a few of these, such as William Lane's *50 Proverbs: Traditional and Christian Wisdom*, used a somewhat similar design that showed how the heritage of traditional proverbs can be adapted for Christian use. However, as far as we know these are the first proverb books specifically designed both as textbooks for pastoral training centers and as resource books for pastors and other church educators.

Though the grant-funded period of our Project ended in 1997, the ripple effects of these books may spread out in many ways in years to come. For example, faculty who use the textbooks in their local language could supplement them with proverbs and notes of their own, or they could require each graduating student to submit five or ten more proverbs with notes and explanations. These additional proverbs could be published in booklet form as a gift of the graduating class to the entire church or serially in a church paper or be adapted for use on radio.

For examination purposes, faculty could set ten proverbs and require students to write short essays on two or three of them, showing how they would abuse these proverbs in preaching. Conversely, faculty could set a Scripture passage and ask students to write down and explain proverbs which could be used when preaching on it. By such methods they would be training a new generation to draw on their own cultural resources instead of merely on Western theological textbooks. Also school curriculums promoting mother-tongue can easily use these series of proverbs as a source of wisdom for teaching.

Another possibility is that the English translations of these three books may serve as an inspiration and model for other African writers working in their own languages. Whether they follow the pattern of this series precisely or adapt it to fit better in their own situations, they would be doing a great service to the Church. They are helping Christians work out a Christ-pleasing way of relating the new gospel to the old traditions.

Still another great possibility for the books is for use by black pastors in the Caribbean, North America and Europe. The books enable these pastors to tap ancient African wisdom and profit from the devotional reflections of current African writers as they prepare sermons for people interested in the world from which their forebears were uprooted.

The books might even enlighten a few whites in the West. As a white American who lived in Africa long enough to learn an African language (Sesotho), let me say that African wisdom has not yet received the respect it deserves in the West. If we ask where Africa has influenced current American culture, the common answer would be in the areas of popular music and professional sports, not in the area of thought and wisdom.

It is not that Africa has no intellectual contribution to make to the world – far from it. The problem is that the West has not yet learned to recognize deep wisdom in the form of concrete proverbs rather than abstract philosophical treatises. Will whites begin to recognize brilliant, deep wisdom in proverbs by reading these books? One hopes so but even if they do not, it is not a criticism of the books or the writers. The books will rightly be judged by their impact on Africans and people of African heritage.

News about these and other developments in this field is available on the Internet at www.afriprov.org, a web site run from Tanzania and Kenya to promote attention to African proverbs and stories. Much of God's wisdom and guidance for Africans has been given to them in the form of proverbs, and those who are interested in passing God's word to the next generation should not despise or neglect these gifts. As the Akan proverb says, "You do not point to the ruins of your father's village with the left hand."

Stan Nussbaum, Coordinator
African Proverbs Project

Acknowledgements

For a number of years I have had an interest in oral tradition and related problems, although I am not a specialist. In October, 1995, I was fortunate enough to attend a Symposium on the "African Proverb in the Twenty-First Century", held at the University of South Africa (UNISA), in Pretoria. There, I was asked to participate in the Africa Proverbs Project as one of the writers of the proverbs for teaching and preaching, based on the "Lakeside Tonga" oral literature in Malawi.

First, I must thank Rev. Dr. Stan Nussbaum (Coordinator) and Rev. Joshua Kudadjie (Editor), and of course all the members of the African Proverbs Project Committee, for willingly accepting me to be one of the writers in this very challenging and important activity. I also thank The Pew Charitable Trusts in Philadelphia who provided the funds that made it possible for me to write and publish this book.

I realised that this task needed much patience, as the Tonga proverb would say, *"Kuwona maso gha Nkhono nkhudeka"* (If you want to see a snail's eyes, you need to be patient). The saying is true. It needed much patience for me to go round the Tonga villages to come up with a normative anthology of these proverbs through interviews. Thus, the process in producing the proverbs was a complex one, checking while listening to original tapes, reading through the transcripts, marking the important proverbs, translating them into English, arranging them in their alphabetical order. In fact, the whole process of analysing was not an easy task.

Since the Tonga say, *"Chikumbu chimoza kuti chituswa nyinda cha"* (One thumb does not squash a louse), I further asked a number of trustworthy friends to discuss with them the meanings of some of the proverbs. These resource persons include: Messrs. Kanyama Chiwiwi Mwasi (T/A, Chiwiwi II); Richard Godfrey Chiya Phiri; Bright Zgawowa Mphande; John Chikuse Chirwa; Goldon Nyirenda; Sam Kandodo Banda (MP); T.C. Katenga Kaunda; Mr. Stack Banda; Chief Munchindwi (VH); Chief Malanda (TA), Chief Malenga Mzoma (T/A); Chief Fuka-Mapile (T/A); Chief Msundu (GVH); Chief Chivuta (GVH); Mrs. Annisty Kamanga; Miss Maria Banda; Mrs. Martha Nyirenda; Miss Lini Nyamanda (VH); Rev. Wesley Manda; Rev. Charles Blackmore Banda; Rev. Flywel Chimwembe Mwale and Rev. Dr. William Manda, who also very kindly edited the Tonga proverbs. To all these I say, *"Mugonenge kutali ndi Moto"* (Keep away from fire). For the resource persons who passed away before seeing the birth of this book, *"Chiuta wasunge Mizimu yinu ndi kugona mu chimango"* (May God keep your souls and rest in peace).[1]

Professor Dr. Dan Chimwenje, then Director of Malawi Institute of Education) deserves grateful acknowledgment for kindly releasing me to attend the Symposium in Pretoria where I was exposed to this precious work and also for giving me some time to visit the field in order to collect this material.

I dedicate this book to Mary my own wife, who tirelessly typed original manuscripts, and our children for their patience, understanding and cooperation. Also to my late father and mother for their unceasing love and care during my boyhood, who through the filter of folktales, legends, proverbs and riddles helped to lay the foundations for my endeavour to explore our African way of life.

I thank the Almighty God that I have been able to participate in this noble task, in order to preserve our Tonga cultural heritage. If something has been done in a hurry or omitted from this book, it is my fault.

Assoc. Prof. Rev. David Kapanyela Mphande, DipTh; BTh; MST; PhD,
Mzuzu, Malawi, January, 2006

---

[1] Some of these respondents have passed away, since 1994. When I did my research. May their should rest in peace.

Series Introduction

Joshua N. Kudadjie, Series Editor

The people of every race or culture have their own modes of communicating among themselves. Some of these modes are the song, art, sculpture, and drumming. But by far the most commonly used mode is verbal language. There are different forms of verbal language; for instance, common language, idiom, secret or esoteric language, and the proverb. This book is concerned with one class of proverbs: traditional African proverbs.

A. General Features of African Proverbs

Much of the language and thought of Africans are expressed in proverbs. In many ways, African traditional proverbs are just like those of the people of other cultures and races. Like others, African proverbs are short sayings which contain the wisdom and experiences of the people of old. Although there are also long proverbs—which look more like short stories or poems—the overwhelming majority of African proverbs are short, pithy statements.

African proverbs usually have two meanings: the literal or primary meaning, and the deeper or real meaning. The real meaning of African proverbs is not always apparent. This is precisely why they are called proverbs. For instance, the Ghanaian Akan, Dangme and Ga expressions for "to cite a proverb," *bu abe*, means "to bend," "curve," or "twist words," to make them complicated. Similarly, the Lugbara (Uganda) term that is used to designate proverbs, *e'yo obeza*, literally means "mixed words," "twisted speech" or "indirect talk." The meaning of a proverb is not fixed, and so it can be modified. The user is free to reconstruct a proverb in order to make it appropriate in the particular context in which it is being used. To modify a proverb, one may delete, paraphrase, elaborate or transfer elements in it. The hearer must be witty to interpret and grasp the meaning of a proverb.

Another important feature of African proverbs is that for a proverb to be appropriate when cited, the situation depicted in the primary meaning as well as its deeper meaning must match that of the context and situation to which it is being applied. Take, for instance, the Bassa proverb: "An elder knows where to locate a crab's heart." The proverb is pointing to difficult and complex problems whose solution can hardly be imagined. They are like a crab's heart which can hardly be located. Yet in both cases an elder has the solution: from his store of knowledge and experience he can locate a crab's heart; and from his experience and wisdom, coupled with patience and careful scrutiny, he can get to the root of a complex problem and offer solutions. This characteristic of the African proverb and its application calls for a technique that comes with long periods of training and practice, whether formal or informal. Similarly, to understand a proverb correctly is also a task, and calls for discernment; for those who hear the proverbs do not always understand them. This is because the truths and advice expressed in the proverbs are not always stated in plain common language but rather in figures of speech, metaphors and images. Sometimes, things that are alike or opposites are compared and contrasted. One needs to reason and use the imagination in order to get their real meaning.

B. Source and Authority

In Africa, proverbs are not usually ascribed to any particular individual, but collectively to the ancestors, the wise men and women of old. In most cases, it is not known who composed a particular proverb. But whether known or not, all proverbs are credited to the elders of old, even if a particular composer is still alive. In many African societies, when a proverb is cited, it is preceded with a statement like, "So said the elders." This may be a way of according proverbs authority. It is also a way of saying that all the people own the proverbs, and that they contain experience, wisdom, and valid counsel which are to be acknowledged by all. Thus, the collective thought, beliefs, and values of an African people can be discerned from their proverbs.

C. Scope and Content

There are thousands, perhaps millions, of African proverbs. New ones are still composed, and old ones are adapted or given new meanings to suit new situations. Anyone who is ingenious—that is, one who is creative, observant and has the ability to reflect and deduce a moral lesson from common happenings—can compose a proverb.

African proverbs contain observations gathered from common everyday events and experiences concerning the nature, life and behaviour of human beings as well as those of animals, birds, plants, and other natural objects; and even supernatural objects and beings. Some of the proverbial sayings are statements of historical facts about the people, while others contain information about their culture. For instance, the Ewe proverb, "When Nôtsie chief sends you to war, you yourself have to find a way of hiding from your enemies," tells of events in their history some 600 years ago when many Ewe lost their lives in wars that they fought for the chief of Nôtsie (an ancient walled city situated in present-day Togo). A great number of them express their philosophical thoughts, religious beliefs and values. The Akan proverbial saying that "God pounds *fufu* for the one-handed person" is a theological statement of their experience of God's provision, loving kindness and gracious dealings with humankind.

Other proverbs reflect the social structure of traditional African societies. For example, there are proverbs that suggest how to deal with elders, children, a spouse and so on, and there are some which indicate the position and role of various members of the society. The Ga proverb: "When a woman rears a goat, it is a man who slaughters it," shows the position and role of the woman in Ga traditional society as a subordinate but indispensable companion and partner of the man. Similarly, the Dangme proverb "The stream side drinking gourd does not make one die of thirst" (i.e., it saves one from dying of thirst), shows the importance of women in the created order; for it means that a man who has a wife at home will not die of hunger. At a deeper level, it means that a man finds his complement, his fulfillment in woman, a wife.

A close look at African traditional proverbial sayings shows clearly that the main concerns expressed in the proverbs relate to every aspect of human life. The ultimate purpose of the proverbs is to teach wisdom and moral lessons. Thus they contain, and are used to convey, moral lessons and advice on how to live a good and prosperous life.

The proverbs touch on all conditions of life: wealth and poverty, health and sickness, joy and sorrow; occupations: farming, hunting, fishing, building, trading, and so on; and other kinds of activity: healing, cooking, walking, sleeping, marriage, childbearing, upbringing, etc. There are proverbs which speak about and to all manner of people: kings and citizens, nobles and slaves, women and men, children and adults, apprentices and master craftsmen, and so on.

African proverbs contain observations and good counsel against undesirable vices like anger, backbiting, greed, ingratitude, laziness, lying, pride, procrastination, selfishness, stealing and so forth. The Ugandan proverb, "Anger killed a mother cow," warns against anger, while the South African proverb, "Horns which are put on do not stick properly," condemns hypocrisy and arrogance. Many other proverbs also praise and advise people to cultivate virtues that promote progress and ensure well-being; as for instance, circumspection, co-operation, gratitude, humility, patience, perseverance, prudence, respect and unity. The Igbo proverbs, "The palm wine tapper does not say everything he sees from the top of the palm tree," and "If the mouth says the head should be beheaded, when it is beheaded, the mouth follows it," both teach prudence and the need not to speak just anyhow or say everything one sees or knows.

D. Context and Use

In traditional African society, one can hardly hear anyone speak a few sentences without citing a proverb. For the initiated, the citing of proverbs comes naturally without any conscious or special effort. This is as true during ordinary conversation as during formal and solemn discourse. However, proverbs tend to be more purposely cited during serious or formal discourse, such as during proceedings of the council of elders, a chief's court, an arbitration, family meetings, or during exhortations on how to live a morally good life.

A cursory examination may suggest that some proverbs contradict others. For example, some proverbs counsel self-reliance, while others counsel community effort. The truth, however, is that in their own contexts and particular situations, each is apt. In real life situations, too, there are paradoxes and apparent contradictions. For instance, in certain situations, the best thing to do is to be silent, while in others, speaking out is the wise thing to do. Thus, although silence and speaking out may appear conflicting when put together, in the appropriate contexts, each is positive. It is no wonder, then, that since proverbs relate to real life situations, they sometimes seem to conflict with each other; but they are only apparent and not real contradictions. This fact underscores the need to use proverbs in the right context and appropriate situation.

It is also important to note that one proverb can have several meanings and can, therefore, be applied to different situations. For instance, the Ga proverb, "If you want to send a message to God, tell it to the wind," can be used in different situations: to teach that God is everywhere; to teach one the correct Ga procedure that if you want to see the chief, you must first see the linguist; or to advise that if you have a bothersome matter that you cannot speak out, you have to tell it to those who can pass it on.

On the other hand, in some cases, many different proverbs teach the same moral lesson, and can, thus, be used for emphasis. The Ga people say: "A kitchen that leaks (or a shed in ruins) is better than a thicket." The Ewe have a proverb which says, "Even a good-for-nothing fellow can carry a pot of palm wine to the funeral." The Dangme say: "Mud-water also can be used to quench fire." All these proverbs teach the same moral lesson, namely, that every person is of some use; therefore, everyone should be given due regard, and people should have a sense of their own worth and be contented with what they are.

African proverbs can be used for several purposes. They can be used for the linguistic analysis of a particular language or dialect. Historical information as well as the thought, customs, beliefs and values of a society can also be obtained through their proverbs. Besides, African proverbs are a literary device used to embellish speech. This is because many of the idioms of an African language are embedded in its proverbs. As it were, African proverbs are used as sweeteners to communicate effectively. As one Ga writer (E.A. Nee-Adjabeng Ankra) put it, speaking without citing proverbs is like eating soup that has no salt in it. Proverbs are cited to confirm, reinforce or modify a statement; or to heighten and attract attention to a point or message; or simply to summarize a speech. Sometimes, too, they are used to communicate a fact or opinion which it might be impolite or even offensive to state in direct speech or plain language. They are also used to make people appreciate speech, or facilitate understanding, and lead to conviction. As one Yoruba observation has it: "A proverb is the horse which can carry one swiftly to the discovery of ideas."

Although all these uses are important, they are, in fact, means to an end. The ultimate purpose of proverbs is to impart wisdom; teach good moral and social values; warn against foolish acts; provide a guide to good conduct; and to influence people's conduct and help them to succeed in life.

E. African Proverbs and the Mission of the Church

African proverbs can be extremely useful and effective for all these purposes, particularly as a tool for teaching moral and social values, and how to conduct oneself successfully in the business of life. They are short and not easily forgettable. They are also popular for their humour. Moreover, they provoke vivid images in the mind, such that things that are otherwise abstract and difficult to grasp become relatively easy to understand.

Proverbs have the power to change people's conduct, because the truths portrayed in them are so plain and unchallengeable that those who understand the morals and advice they contain, feel compelled to conduct their lives in the manner prescribed in the proverbs by the wise elders of old.

It cannot be doubted that desiring to live the good life is not enough, for one can know and even will to do good, and still be unable to do it (see Romans 7:14-25). It is those who accept the gospel of Jesus Christ and have the Holy Spirit in them who have power to do the good. Yet, it is important to note that Jesus Christ who brought this new power to work from within a person, himself also used the method of influencing people from the outside by appealing to their minds and hearts through teaching. In doing this, he used stories and proverbial sayings. There can be no doubt, then, that the present-day Church may attain its goal (which is to make all peoples the followers of Christ and teach them to obey what he has commanded), if it encourages the proper use of proverbial sayings. In using these indigenous proverbial sayings, however, the Church must correct and replace what is not so good in them, and add on from the Scriptures what is more excellent.

At this point in Africa's history when there are cries everywhere for moral and social reform, the use of proverbs in moral education is urgent. The many positive features of African proverbs, such as those cited above, make them most invaluable and unavoidable as instruments of teaching. The Church which has always been interested in people living the morally good life, must use African proverbs even more earnestly, especially in preaching and teaching. Their use will help immensely to teach the truths of many biblical themes and stories, and to affect the moral, social and spiritual lives of the people for the better; for when a proverb is used correctly, it speaks to the intellect, the soul and the heart—that is, to the understanding, the feelings and the will. Over the centuries, African proverbs have successfully done this. They can, thus, be used to great advantage in Christian preaching and teaching.

Part I

A Christian Framework for Using Tonga Proverbs (Nthanthi/Nthalika)

1. The Lakeside Tonga People and their Language

By David K. Mphande

There is much wealth of knowledge and wisdom from the Tonga oral litera-ture. The 194 proverbs collected in this book for teaching and preaching, as well as the additional 116 in Appendix A, are just a representative of one aspect of the genres of the Tonga traditional narratives. To understand Tonga literature, one must also know something of Tonga culture. It is not too diffi-cult to make the distinction between the unwritten and the written literature of the Tonga people, though very little or none is in written form, since the oral or verbal literature is still being transmitted from one generation to another.

This chapter is concerned with the concepts and values of the Tonga peo-ple which include: their genesis; the importance of kinship as represented in their institutional form of the extended family system, expressed in their proverb, *Kase-ruta-Kase-weku*, meaning, "What you expect others to do for you, do for them also"; the ability to produce a child as a necessary factor for the continuance of marriage, as expressed in their proverb, *Nyoli yizilwa ndi mavungwa* (A chicken is dignified by feathers); a person is respected because of his/her idea of the existence of God as source of life and to Him also life goes back, as expressed in the proverb, *Chiuta wamto* (God has taken him); the belief in ancestral spirits as though the dead were still living, since the family relationship continues, as in the proverb, *Wakuya ku muzi ukuru* (He has gone to the great city), meaning, "He has joined the majority" and so on.

The familial, political, educational, economic and religious spheres of life as part and parcel of the whole Tonga culture are reflected in their oral lit-erature. Within this framework the chapter explores the Tonga habitat, ven-ues of moral instruction, and an examination of the thematic approach to the proverbs.

A. Their Origin and Connections

The Lakeside Tonga[2] people of Malawi, in Nkhata Bay district, share in the Bantu history to which their ancestors belonged. This history is dominated

---

[2] J. van Velsen (1964). *The Politics of Kinship: A Study in Social Manipulation among the Lakeside Tonga of Nyasaland*: Manchester University Press. Van Velsen uses the term

by change. It is marked at times by slow expansion and at others by rapid migration. Their great ingenuity is shown in the ways they learned to adapt to different environments; modifying lifestyle and culture accordingly. The account of their creativity and enterprise is extraordinary. The religious development is equally fascinating. Most historians would see the Tonga people as of heterogeneous origin. A description of the Tonga people quoted by J. van Velsen goes like this:

> The Tonga have had a reputation with these visitors for being "intelligent but truculent ... and difficult of management", quarrelling amongst themselves ... and mutual jealousies and ambitions which kept the country in fever of unrest; conceited and truculent, undisciplined and fond of intrigue; the most prominent of all tribes in Nyasaland both for intelligence and disputes; a remarkable people, highly intelligent and having a degree of independence seldom encountered elsewhere in Africans. This is but a small selection from many similar comments.[3]

J. van Velsen has also noted that the beginnings of the Tonga nation probably lie in the decades of the eighteenth century. This was the period of the penetrations of ivory trading groups from across the northeastern shores of Lake Nyasa and the tribal movements in the northern parts of what is now Malawi. Some groups settled in Tongaland. It is however believed that the Tonga came from the same place as the Chewa and Tumbuka. People who believe in the latter conclusion possibly see some similarities in Chichewa and Tumbuka names found in Chitonga (e.g. Phiri, Banda, Mwale, Nkhoma, etc.) and the presence of many similar words. For instance, the chart below shows the similarities in languages:

Chichewa	Chitumbuka	Chitonga	English
Nthanu	Chidokoni	Nthanu	Folktale/story
Mai/mama	Mama	Ama	Mother
Atate/tate	Adada/dada	Ada	Father
Nkhoswe	Nkhoswe	Nkhoswe	A go-between
Kuitana	Kuchema	Kudana	To call
Mwamuna	Mwanarume	Munthurume	Man
Mwana	Mwana	Mwana	Child
Fodya	Foja/Hona	Foja	Tobacco
Nsima	Sima	Sima	Thick porridge

"Lakeside Tonga People" in order to differentiate them from the Tonga of Lower Shire around the Zambezi valley and the Tonga of Zambia.
[3] Quoted by van Velsen, *The Politics of Kinship*, p.1.

What seems to be most likely, is that the Tonga had good relationships with the Tumbuka and Chewa with whom they intermarried. These similarities are also for linguistic styles, since the Tonga share in the Bantu cultural unity. The Tonga themselves have their legend which depicts their origin as from the north. Karonga Mzizi and Chiwiwi are the heroes. The different names of the people were developed according to the habit each clan liked to follow.[4]

B. Their Habitat

The Tonga live in small clusters of houses scattered through the bush and the forests, among the rivers and streams and by the lakeshore. Most villages are small, often 20-50 houses. These grouped compact clusters of thatched huts and few iron-roofed houses constitute Tonga villages. The villages are the most common settings for the various stories told by the men and women as they sit relaxed in their homes in the evenings. It is therefore important to understand something of their appearance and significance.

The distribution of the population is determined by the geographical features of Tongaland. In fact, along parts of the lakeshore the population is more concentrated than in the hill regions. As one gets farther inland from the lakeshore plains, the population becomes less concentrated, and the distance between one group of hamlets and another may be greater. Some villages are reached by steep winding paths up which both visitors and residents must negotiate to reach their settled community at the top, and which the women travel many times daily with their water containers balanced on their heads from a well or a running stream below the hill.

The staple crop of the Tonga is cassava. The cultivation of cassava requires comparatively little hard labour and can be done entirely by women. Cassava is normally served as a thick porridge (*sima*) together with a side dish of relish (*dende*). The favourite relish consists of chicken, beef or fish. This is the kind of relish which every hostess strives to offer her visitors. Their respect of a visitor is implied in the proverb, *Mlendo ndi dungwi* (A visitor is like dew), meaning, a visitor should not be a bother for he/she is but for a short time. Birds and insects fill the rain-forest with sounds of all kinds. Monkeys and baboons live in the trees where they find food in plenty.

---

[4] This information was obtained from an unpublished document written by the late Filemon Kamnkhwala Chirwa on the "Genesis of Tonga people". It has also been confirmed by Mr. Kanyama Chiwiwi Mwasi (TA) the grand-grandson of Karonga Mzizi. The legend was also told by Mr. Richard Chiya Phiri. They all believe that the legend is their true traditional history. The full version is not recorded here.

This explains why many Tonga myths and folktales depict common topics about the talking birds, snakes and animals. There are also stories about hunters. A proverb which relates to monkeys says, *Pusi wakukota waliskika ndi wana wake* (Grand-monkey is fed by her children) meaning, aging parents need to be cared for by children.

C. Venues for Moral Instruction

The Tonga word for a net-shelter is *khumbi* but this refers only to the structure, if the net-shelter is also the place where men often sit together, they will call it *mphara*. Of course, the community life of the Tonga revolves round the *mphara*. In most cases the *mphara* is the men's open place in a village. *Mphara* also means a court or any other ad hoc meeting of men trying to decide on a specific problem, for example, discussions on funerals or divorce. It is a place where men weave baskets, make mats and hoe handles, play *nchuwa* (drafts), *mbela* (teetotums), *mangolongondo* (wooden musical instruments) and games; while young men sit there to learn various arts and crafts and run errands.

Mphara life is also a source of disciplining the young. Here, young people acquire on a general or collective basis, information concerning themselves. Here again children would listen to songs, folktales, proverbs, riddles, jokes, etc. containing dynamic moral messages. Through these media the younger members of the society absorb the ideas that will guide them through life.

At the women's open place (*paduli*), or pounding place, the women likewise play their games, sing songs, dance, gossip, hear and settle disputes, pound cassava for flour and work on arts and crafts, such as making pots, *visaku* (fish traps) and so on. When night falls, young women sleep in *nthanganene* (girls' dormitory), while young men sleep in *mphara* (the young unmarried men's quarters). It must be emphasized here that the *mphara*, *nthanganene* and *visenga* are the early settings for moral development in the young people's rites of passage, in the Tonga society.

D. Forms and Nature of Tonga Literature

So far very little has been written and printed on Tonga oral literature. Moreover, everyday situations arise in which the Tonga employ stories, proverbs, riddles, aphorisms, songs, rituals and taboos. The Tonga oral traditional literature consists mostly of *Nthanu* (folktales/myths). These are the most significant literary forms of narratives. *Nthanthi/Vituwu* (Proverbs) ranks next. Other forms include *Vindawi* (riddles), *Sumu* (songs), *Gule* (dance), *Mwambu* (rituals) and *Vinguzgu* (taboos). The basic oral drama is the *Malipenga* dance for boys and young men, and *Chioda* for women and girls.

E. Emphases of Tonga Proverbs

The proverbs collected show the Tonga philosophical outlook, religious and moral conceptions for revealing their values, philosophy, character, wisdom, beliefs and practices. In some cases they clearly express the deepest-set values of the Tonga people, showing the drive that motivates moral behaviour in the people. They reveal concepts of a human being, society, the world and God. Like folktales, they address several themes such as unity and cooperation, responsibility, conflict, obedience and disobedience, good and evil, etc. A representation of such themes is shown below.

1. The Defenceless People who Need Protection

The term defenseless is used to describe unknown travellers, the needy, aging parents, children, the infirm, orphans, madmen and women. Thus, as noted earlier, the traveller calling at the home should always be well treated because, *Mulendo ndi dungwi*, in crude translation, a visitor is dew. The traveller or stranger or visitor is compared to dew because in the tropics, dew is seen in the mornings of certain months only for a short spell of time. The traveller likewise is not a permanent bother to the host.

In discussing about aging the Tonga have this proverb, *Nyoko ndi nyoko nanga wapunduki* (Your mother is your mother even if she happens to be lame). This reflects the thought that aging parents need protection and care. Concerning children the Tonga say, *Mwana wamunyako ndisamba m'manja wako ndi ryangako* (Your neighbour's child is told, "wash your hands", yours is told "you eat"), meaning you ask your neighbour's child to go and wash his/her hands when you tell your child to sit down and eat, etc.

2. On Unity and Cooperation

The Tonga people encourage unity, although some Europeans have stated that the Tonga practise individualism. For instance, they cite proverbs such as *Cho chiwengi pano nchakutose* (Whatever happens here, happens to us all), or *Wawi mbanthu yo weyija ndi nyama* (Two are people, which is alone is an animal), or *Chawona munyako charutapo mawa che pako* (What your neighbour has seen is gone, tomorrow it will see you). All these three proverbs show that a person is not an island in Tonga society. They talk about the need to unite or share things together.

3. On Conflict in Family or Community

When the Tonga talk about conflict or quarrelling between persons they say, *Vimiti vyakume pamoza vipamba cha ng'wema* (Trees which grow near each other cannot avoid brushing against each other), or *Matako ghawi ghapamba cha ku kwenthana* (Two buttocks do not fail to make a friction). Indeed people are aware of the rubbing and brushing together of personalities which exist, where unhealthy atmosphere of fear, distrust and suspicion often reigns.

4. On the Concept of Wrong and Retribution

Wrong is conceived by the Tonga people as offending one's fellow human being who is both a brother/sister and a child of God (Chiuta/Mulungu). Thus God becomes annoyed when people do evil things. If there is an outbreak of disease in the community, people use the proverb *Kwawiya Chiuta* meaning, God is inflicting the people with disease or God is punishing the people. Sometimes if one has injured another in the case of witchcraft they say *Jisu ku jisu* meaning, an eye for an eye. This is a Biblical principle of Mosaic Law.

5. On God's Providence and Care

The Tonga believe that God (i.e. *Chiuta/Mulungu*) is *Chandu* (The Beginner), *Mlengi, Mlenga, Mulenga Charu* (The Maker or World Maker) *Chata* (Creator). As the Preserver, God is variously known as *Mlimiliya* (The Keeper), *Mlerawana* (The Nourisher), and so on. God's abode is expressed in a proverb which says, *Chiuta wa kuchanya* (The God of heaven). A nice person is said to be *Kana kaku Chiuta* (i.e. a little child of the Wonderful), etc. Thus when referring to death they say, *Chiuta wamto* (God has taken him/her). All these expressions, titles and attributes of God show how the Tonga people believe in the High God as the source of life and giver of all good things including rain, hence God is referred to as *Mlenga-vuwa* (Rain-Maker). So the rainbow is regarded as *Uta waku Chiuta* (The bow of God).

F. Conclusion

The six representative themes discussed above show that the Tonga people employ proverbs as patterns of symbolic reference for analysing issues brought for consultation, serving as highly symbolic language to explain problems of existence. Many of the proverbs as shall be seen in the anthology in chapter four perform the function of illustrating various moral, religious and philosophical issues relating to people. The proverbs are based upon common experience presented in symbolic terms, and they are statements of life. Proverbs in a way have a didactic intent.

It was therefore observed during field visits that the propounding and expounding of proverbial wisdom was associated with the older people, primarily men. Therefore, as in written literature, symbols are widely employed in various forms of Tonga literature for probing deep philosophical, moral and spiritual matters. They are a mark of high artistic sophistication in Tonga oral culture.

2. Emphases of Biblical Proverbs

by Joshua N. Kudadjie, Series Editor

A. Introduction

Proverbs and proverbial sayings have been used in both the Old and New Testaments. They can be found in various books of the Bible—for example, in Ezekiel 16:44 ("Like mother, like daughter."); Ezekiel 18:2 ("The parents ate the sour grapes, but the children got the sour taste."); 2 Peter 2:22 ("A dog goes back to what it has vomited."). However, the best known is the collection of proverbs in the Book of Proverbs and some in Ecclesiastes. Jesus also used extensively in his teaching some kind of proverbial sayings, commonly called parables.

Apart from the parables of Jesus which are usually long, and a few other long ones in the Book of Proverbs, the proverbs used in the Bible are short, easily remembered statements. They contain truths gathered from life's experiences. Examples of the long parables are: the parable of the unforgiving servant (Matthew 18:21-35), the parable of the tenants in the vineyard (Matthew 21:33-46), and the parable of the talents (Matthew 25:14-30). There are also a few fairly long proverbs in the Book of Proverbs; for instance, 6:6-11: the ant and the sluggard; 24:2-6: the vineyards of a lazy man.

B. The Sources of Biblical Proverbs

In their present form, the bulk of biblical proverbs have been ascribed to specific individuals; namely, King Solomon (Proverbs 1:1), Agur (Proverbs 30:1), the mother of King Lemuel (Proverbs 31:1), and Jesus Christ (Matthew 13:1-3).

In Bible times, proverbs were composed by wise men, and were widely used in Israelite society and among other ancient peoples. King Solomon, for example, acclaimed to be wiser than the wise men of the East and Egypt—indeed, acclaimed to be the wisest of all men—is said to have composed three thousand proverbs (1 Kings 4:29-33, see also Ecclesiastes 1:1; 12:9).

Solomon and the other composers of proverbs formulated their proverbs from life's experiences. These experiences were based on their observation of human life and behaviour, animals, birds, reptiles, and fish (1 Kings 4:33). Solomon is said to have been given his unusual wisdom and insight by God himself (1 Kings 4:29).

From the parables of Jesus—which are a kind of extended proverbs—four sources can be discerned:

(i)   observations from the world of nature: for example, the parable of the sower (Mark 4:1-9); the parable of the seed growing secretly (Mark 4:26-29);

(ii)   knowledge of familiar customs of everyday life and events: like the parable of the yeast (Matt. 13:33); the parable of the ten virgins (Matt. 25:1-13);

(iii) from well-known events in recent history: e.g., the parable of the high-ranking man about to be made king but who was not liked by some of the citizens, and who gave gold coins to his servants to trade with (Luke 19:12-27); (historians have identified this person to be Archelaus, son of Herod the Great); and

(iv)   from normal probable events, as in the parables of the labourers in the vineyard (Matthew 20:1-16); the prodigal son (Luke 15 11-32), and the unjust judge (Luke 18:2-8).

C. The Form, Structure and Style of Biblical Proverbs

As has already been stated, some of the proverbial sayings in the Bible are rather extensive. But most of them are short. The Hebrew word for "proverb" comes from a word which means "to be like." Thus, often in the Book of Proverbs, the message of a proverb is given by comparing two things and showing how they are similar in some respect. For example, "An idea well-expressed is like a design of gold, set in silver" (Proverbs 25:11), or "People who promise things that they never give are like clouds and wind that bring no rain" (25:14).

Another style commonly used in Proverbs is that of contrast, showing the difference between two things. This is common in chapters 10-15. For example, "A gracious lady is respected, but a woman without virtue is a disgrace" (11:16), or, again, "Sensible people keep quiet about what they know, but stupid people advertise their ignorance" (12:23).

Sometimes conditional statements are used. For instance, "If you repay good with evil, you will never get evil out of your house" (17:13), and "Get good advice and you will succeed; don't go charging into battle without a plan" (20:18).

Another feature is the use of parables, such that behind what seems to be one plain truth lies another, deeper or more general truth. For instance, the proverb, "Never eat more honey than you need; too much may make you vomit" (Prov. 25:16), is saying something true about honey. But it is also a general warning not to indulge in too much pleasure, lest one becomes fed up or ends up in disgrace.

Similar styles are used by Jesus in his parables. The kingdom of heaven is as invaluable as a piece of land with hidden treasure, describing the need to sacrifice everything else in order to possess it (Matthew 13:44); and if you want to enter the kingdom of God, you must not defer the decision to accept the invitation, as portrayed in the parable of the wedding feast (Matthew 22:1-4).

D. Purpose of the Proverbs

The Book of Proverbs is quite clearly a guidebook to successful living, especially to young people, as the opening verses declare:

> Here are proverbs that will help you to recognize wisdom and good advice and understand sayings with deep meaning. They can teach you how to live intelligently and how to be honest, just, and fair. They can make an inexperienced person clever and teach young men how to be resourceful. These proverbs can even add to the knowledge of wise men and give guidance to the educated, so that they can understand the hidden meanings of proverbs and the problems that wise men raise (Proverbs 1:2-6 TEV).

The one who heeds the voice of wisdom as revealed in the proverbs, and avoids the temptations listed, is assured the rewards of long and pleasant life, wealth, honour and happiness (Proverbs 3:16-17).

E. The Most Emphasized Themes

We summarize the teaching on nine of the most emphasized themes in biblical proverbs. We have limited the sources to the Book of Proverbs and the Parables of Jesus. The facts stated and observations made in the themes are truths that must be made known to all who desire knowledge about life. The instructions and advice given contain basic unchanging principles which, if heeded, can make one wise and guide one to live an acceptable and successful life; for they emphasize wisdom, understanding, insight, intelligence, discipline, honesty, justice, righteousness, goodness and fairness.

1. God

For the Hebrew, like other ancient people, nothing can be more real than God. To handle things properly and succeed in life, one must understand the nature and ways of things, and the universal laws that operate behind them. Such understanding comes only from God, the maker of all things. That is why the Hebrew wise man declares from the very beginning of the discourse on successful living, that "The fear of the Lord is the beginning of wisdom" (Proverbs 1:7). That is the very first step in successful living. To fear God is to remember him and show proper regard for him. A person who wishes to do that, is advised, as it were, to practise the presence of God, not only sometimes or in some things only, but in all things and at all times. If one is thus conscious of God, relying not on his or her own thoughts, but trusting God with all his or her heart—at home, work, in politics, etc—God will show him or her the right way (3:5-6). Thus all he or she does will be according to God's will, and, since it is God's will that in the end prevails (19:21), the one who relies on God will succeed.

If a person has experienced how reliable God is, he would avoid doing anything that could spoil his relationship with God, such as lying, disowning or disgracing God. He would pray constantly that God may deliver him from any conditions of life that could lead to such denial or dishonour, as for example, extreme riches which would make him proud; or extreme poverty that might make him steal (30:7-9). So his prayer would be, "give me only as much food as I need" (30:8).

Another important truth that the ancient Hebrew wise man learnt is that a nation without God's guidance is a nation without order; but happy is the one who keeps God's law (29:18). How true, and how much this counsel needs to be heeded today, both in the lives of individuals and of nations!

2. The Fool

If there is one person who is to be pitied most in life, it is the fool. Going by the description of the Hebrew wise man, a very large number of people in the world are fools—including some of the world's leading scholars, politicians, businessmen and women, and even religious leaders. Among the many characteristics of the fool are the following. He is mentally weak and easily misled (1:10), morally irresponsible and refuses discipline (1:22-32). He has no regard for truth and is satisfied with his own opinion (14:8), does not search for wisdom but speaks nonsense without much thought (15:2, 14); he is proud and dislikes correction and advice (15:12). He is also a fool who is impatient, quarrelsome (12:16; 20:3) and bent on doing evil (17:12). Above all, a person who rejects the Lord is a fool (1:29), for as the Psalmist observes, "the fool says in his heart, 'There is no God.'" (Psalm 53:1-3).

Because of his very nature and his conduct, the fool has nothing good to offer (14:7), and is not liked because of his bad influence, as for instance, in bringing grief and bitter regrets to his very parents (10:1; 17:25).

Just as the fool's greatest vice is rejecting God, so also his greatest punishment for his folly is that God gives him up and has no use for him (3:34). Since he neither gets on with people nor finds favour with God, the fool cannot know true success in life.

3. Various Warnings

There are many warnings not to do things that can destroy one. Four of them are particularly to be noted. Among them is the **warning against joining thieves** (1:8-19). Those who attack and kill and rob others for riches or for the fun of it, "are setting a trap for themselves, a trap in which they will die" (1:18), for "robbery always claims the life of the robber" (1:19).

There are also strong **warnings against adultery** in chapters 5 and 6:20 to 7:27. One is warned to stay away from another man's wife, no matter how beautiful she may be (6:25) or how sweet her lips or smooth her kisses, for they lead to nothing but death (5:3-6). Adultery, experience has shown, is as dangerous as carrying fire against one's chest, or walking on hot coals, and always leads to suffering (6:27-29). A man who commits adultery will lose not only his wealth (5:10; 6:26), but also his honour (5:9,14; 6:33), and his very life (5:9; 6:34-35; 7:26-27). For this reason, one is strongly advised to keep to one's wife alone, and to be completely satisfied with her alone (5:15-19).

Another warning is against **laziness**, for it leads to ruin (24:31-32). The lazy person is known by his many bad habits. He does not start things early but keeps postponing (6:9-10), and when he starts something, he does not finish it (19:24). Because lazy people only think about what they want but do not work for it, they are ruined, and remain helpless and in want (13:4, 21:25-26; 24:31-32). Such people are advised to learn from the way ants live: not waiting to be told what to do, but taking the initiative to plan ahead, work hard while it is possible, and save up for the time of need (6:6-8).

The final warning to note is that against **deceit** which includes: lying, being untruthful and unreliable, disloyalty, making false promises, trickery, hypocrisy, misleading others, and insincere talk that hides what you are really thinking. The experience of the wise has shown without mistake that those who cultivate such evil habits do not get very far in the end; for the Lord God hates such habits (6:1-5, 12-19). Therefore, those who do them end up in destruction; for they are caught in their own traps, and get crushed by the landslides that they themselves start (26:17-28).

In numerous proverbs, the one who desires life is advised to refrain from these evils and, instead, follow the path of wisdom and righteousness wherein is life and success.

4. Wisdom

In a sense all the themes of Proverbs are about wisdom. Yet, the theme of wisdom is treated in a special and detailed way in chapters 1-9. No one can go through life successfully without wisdom, hence the call of wisdom to all (1:20f). Wisdom promises many virtues, including understanding, knowledge, learning, discretion and wise dealing. Through these, one would steer through life and find security, treasures, moral uprightness, etc. (chapter 2) and life itself (4:10; 8:35).

From the observations of the wise men of old, anyone can obtain wisdom, provided he or she is willing to depart from evil (8:13) and the company of ignorant persons (9:4-6), while devoting oneself to wise teachings. If one desires to be wise, one must be determined and teachable (9:9), and accept advice and criticism (13:10; 17:10), especially God's correction (3:11f). But, although training, instruction and discipline can yield wisdom, the real source and ground of wisdom is God—hence the declaration that the fear of the Lord is the beginning of wisdom (2:6). He who seeks wisdom, then, must first seek God.

5. *Friends and Good Neighbours*

God made us human beings to live in community. For community life to be possible, it is necessary, among other things, to have neighbours and friends. But what sort of friend or neighbour? Proverbs gives a detailed description of who may be called a friend. A friend is one who is kind, generous, truthful and reliable (27:10). He would not do anything that would hurt a neighbour (3:29) or spread news of a misunderstanding (25:8-9). He would be silent rather than criticise (11:12) or condemn anyone (14:21). A good friend has tact, knowing when to be close and when to keep his distance; when to say "yes" or "no" (3:27-28); 6:1-5); he does not over-stay his visit (25:17); he knows when a joke is going too far (26:18-19); and he would not do anything that would be inconvenient to a neighbour (27:14).

Besides all this, the good friend must be aware that friendships can be broken and neighbourliness spoilt by bad habits like gossip and doing the wrong thing. Accordingly, he avoids these (16:28; 17:9).

6. *Words*

By word God created the universe. By word Christ healed the sick, raised the dead, and cursed the fig tree. Life in community is hardly possible without words; for through them we communicate and even put our ideas in the minds of other people. With them we praise and pray to God. Such is the power of words that in Proverbs, three of the seven things which the Lord God hates and cannot tolerate have to do with the wrong use of words: lying, evil thought and false witness (6:16-19).

Since words can be used so powerfully for good or ill, the wise men of the ancient near east warned people of their power, and counselled people to use them aright. They advised that one's words must be few, calm and honest. For "the more you talk, the more likely you are to sin" and so the wise keep quiet (10:19). "A gentle answer quietness anger" (15:1), and "Patient persuasion can break down the strongest resistance and can even convince rulers." (25:15) "A good man's words are a fountain of life" (10:11), and a source of wisdom (18:4), while wisely spoken words can heal (12:18). When words are wrongly used by evil and godless people, they can ruin a person (11:9); when used thoughtlessly, they can wound as deeply as any sword (12:18).

Experience has shown, however, that for all their power for good or ill, one needs more than just words to live a good life. For mere words cannot replace hard work (14:23), nor can lies change the truth (26:23-28).

All that Proverbs says about words can be summarized in Paul's advice: "Do not use harmful words, but only helpful words, the kind that build up and provide what is needed, so that what you say will be good to those who hear you." (Ephesians 4:29).

7. The Family

The Hebrew wise men of old recognized the importance of the family as the basic unit of society. As such, they stressed the need for it to be united, for faithfulness within it and for good training of children.

For a family to be good, marriage is to be monogamous and permanent, and couples are to be faithful to each other (5:15-23; 2:16-22). Sexual sin within marriage is evil and dangerous, leading to disgrace and even death (5:9-23), 6:26-35). A husband must love and be faithful to his wife (5:15, 19), while a wife must be generous, good to her husband and contribute to his good standing in society (31:10f).

It is important for parents to speak with one voice and teach what will improve their children's character—such that the children will pay attention to them (1:8-9). Training must begin from early childhood (22:6; 13:24), and is best if it combines both discipline (i.e. the rod, or punishment) and gentle but firm direction (1:9; 13:4; 22:15).

On their part, children are urged again and again to obey their parents and respect them (1:8-9); 4:1), for such obedience is blessed with long and prosperous life (3:2).

Family members and relatives should be helpful and loyal to each other (17:17; 18:24).

Even though sometimes, some children refuse to learn and are disobedient, and some parents also do not give the right training or set a good example, if parents and children follow the advice of the sages of old, as presented in Proverbs, the quality of life in the modern world should be far better than it is now with all the violence, immorality and lawlessness that abound.

8. Life and Death

Another theme emphasized in Proverbs is that of life and death. The words "life" and "death" are used both in their ordinary and figurative senses. Thus, "life" means both living here on earth and a good quality of life. "Death" refers to the physical event of dying, i.e., the end of one's earthly life as well as to a state of conflict in life. In whichever sense one takes it, mature opinion is that all should seek life and avoid death.

If one desires to live and live long, then the way is to be obedient and seek wisdom (3:2; 4:10; 9:11). There are certain conditions and styles of life which add quality to life. For example, close observation has shown that one who finds wisdom finds life (8:35). So also, peace of mind (14:30), honest earning and avoiding bribery give long life (15:27). Again, it is good to be in the favour of those in authority, for that yields blessing, just as clouds give needed rain in spring time (16:15).

On the other hand, certain conditions and experiences are as bad as dying, for people in those states of life have gone astray and missed the way to true life. Consequently, they are in conflict. Such is the case, for example, with the person who is wicked (5:22-23), or has not found wisdom or who hates wisdom (8:36). One can save a child from death and going astray from true life, by timely discipline (23:13-14).

We can escape death and enjoy real life, if we heed these observations and counsels.

9. The Kingdom of God

Outside the ancient Wisdom books of the Old Testament (Job, Proverbs, Ecclesiastes), the most concentrated collection of proverbial sayings in the Bible can be found in the Parables of Jesus, recorded in the Gospels of Matthew, Mark and Luke. There, the major and single theme is the Kingdom of God. We conclude this survey of emphases of biblical proverbs and proverbial sayings with a brief look at these parables.

The collection of Jesus' teachings known as the Sermon on the Mount, ends with a parable of two house builders. One is a fool, for he built on sand, and his house collapsed. The other is a wise person, for he built on rock, and his house survived the storm and the flood (Matthew 6:24-27). Hearing and obeying the teachings of Jesus is like building on rock; it is wisdom and life; while hearing but not obeying the teachings of Jesus is foolishness and death. To Jesus, the wisest thing a person can do is to seek and get into the Kingdom, and the most foolish thing to do is to remain outside it (See Parable of the Ten Virgins, Matthew 25:1-13).

The parables of Jesus teach about a dimension of life that is higher than physical earthly life, or even a good quality of it. They teach about eternal life—life with God, which is the truest life of all; that is life in the Kingdom of God.

When Jesus talked about the Kingdom of God, he did not mean any physical area on earth. Rather, he meant a spiritual realm. In that kingdom, God is the ruler, and his will is done by his subjects (Matthew 6:10); his power is experienced and his Holy Spirit destroys the works of Satan (Luke 11:20). Those who are members of the kingdom have God's Spirit who gives them power to live lives that are noble, righteous, godly, peaceful, joyful, and so on (Romans 14:17; Galatians 5:22-25, etc)

Jesus taught that belonging to this Kingdom is the most important thing. Therefore, one should be prepared to give up everything else in order to get into it. (See parables of the Hidden Treasure and the Pearl in Matthew 13:44-45). The sacrifices that one will have to make may include habits that give benefits but which are ungodly; or a position of authority; or riches, etc. (Matthew 19:16-21; Luke 3:10-14,18; Acts 2:38).

Above all, Jesus revealed that he himself is the one whom the Father has sent to bring the Kingdom to us (Matthew 21:33-46; John 3:16; 4:25-26). He is also the way to God the Father (John 14:6). If a person believes in Jesus and obeys him, that person is abiding in Jesus, and God himself will work in that person to enable him or her to will and to live the kind of life that pleases God (Phil. 2:13). This is the good and truly successful life that both African and biblical proverbs counsel. To live in Jesus, then, is to fulfill the counsels in the proverbs.

3. The Gospel and Tonga Proverbs

The early missionaries came to Tongaland in 1880, when Dr. Robert Laws was given permission by Livingstonia mission to move the whole party to Bandawe from Cape Maclear to be the new settlement of the mission. Later on Alexander G. MacAlpine wrote very little about a systematic study of the Tonga culture. Particular attention was paid to religious beliefs of Tonga and he provided a full account of mortuary rituals.[5] However, his document does not show any interest in the use of Tonga proverbs for preaching and teaching. Yet, from the discussion in chapter one, proverbs if decoded properly are an effective source for discovering people's values, philosophy, character, wisdom, beliefs and practices. The reason is simple. Some early missionaries wanted western values to permeate the African values. In other words, African values were deemed as heathen.

In the Gospels Jesus uses proverbs as guidelines for a good life, moral principles and daily rules. They are exhortations not dogmas. For instance, when Jesus wanted to teach the people on the theme about "God's Kingdom", he used some parable of the Kingdom. Thus, in many occasions, Jesus used proverbs. Here are a few examples from the Bible:

---

[5] A.G. MacAlpine (1905). "Tonga Religious Beliefs and Customs", in the *Aurora.*

- On the theme of the "Kingdom of God" Jesus says, "Many are invited but few are chosen" (*Matthew 22:14*).

- On warning against "hypocrisy", He says, "They are blind leaders of the blind and when one blind man leads another, both fall into a ditch" (*Matthew 15:14*).

- On the theme of "responsibility", Jesus says, "To have good fruit you must have a healthy tree" (*Matthew 12:33*).

- On entering the "Kingdom of God", Jesus says, "No one can break into a strong man's house and take away his belongings unless he first ties up the strong man; then he can plunder his house" (*Matthew 12:29*).

- On "justice" and "reconciliation" the Bible says, "Eye for an Eye and a tooth for a tooth" (*Matthew 5:38*).

- On "showing respect", Jesus says, "A prophet is never welcomed in his hometown" (*Luke 4:24*).

- On "humility", Jesus says, "Whoever wants to be first must place himself last of all and be the servant of all" (*Mark 9:35*).

- On taking "self-initiative", Jesus says, "People who are well do not need a doctor, but only those who are sick" (*Luke 5:32*).

- On the theme of "repentance", Jesus warns: "No one tears a piece of a new coat to patch up an old coat. If he does, he will have torn the new coat, and the piece of new cloth will not match the old. Nor does anyone pour new wine into used wineskins, because the new wine will pour out, and the skins will be ruined" (*Luke 5:36-37*).

- On "making decision", Jesus says, "Foxes have holes and birds have nests, but the Son of Man has no place to lie down and rest" (*Luke 9:58*).

- On "perseverance", Jesus says "Anyone who starts to plow and then keeps looking back is of no use for the Kingdom of God" (*Luke 9:62*).

- On "trust", Jesus says, "A person's true life is not make up of the things he owns, no matter how rich he may be" (*Luke 12:15*).

- On "humility", Jesus says, "For everyone who makes himself great will be humbled and everyone who humbles himself will be make great" (*Luke 14:11*).

♦ On "making choices", Jesus says, "No servant can be the slave of two masters" (*Matthew 6:24*).

♦ On "humility", Jesus says "Who is greater the one who sits down to eat or the one who serves him?" (*Luke 22:27*).

♦ On "disobedience", Jesus says, "Anyone who does evil things hates the light (*John 3:20*).

♦ On "faith", Jesus says, "Who ever eats my flesh and drinks my blood lives in me and I live in him" (*John 6:56*).

♦ On "trust", Jesus says, "People will look at him whom they pierced" (*John 19:37*)

♦ On "obedience", the Bible says, "The one who gathered much did not have too much, and the one who gathered little did not have too little" (*2 Corinthians 8:15* cf. *Exodus 16:18*).

♦ On "responsibility", The Bible says, "The parents ate the sour grapes but the children got the sour taste" (*Jeremiah 31:29*).

Towards the Use of Tonga Proverbs for the Inculturation of the Gospel

Chapter one has revealed how powerful proverbs are as moral and spiritual vehicles. By inculturation is meant incarnating the Gospel in a given cultural context through the way people respond to their religious faith, or the way they celebrate that response in liturgy. As noted above Jesus saw that God's word with its message of salvation would be more meaningful and better understood if he used proverbs, parables or riddles. Likewise the word of God can become more meaningful in as much as it permeates the Tonga culture if preachers can use proverbs.

There are many values that are conveyed through Tonga proverbs which the Gospel affirms as noted above in the teachings of the scriptures. Some of these can be mentioned here that address various themes:

1. Division and Conflicts

Proverb: Mlomu upasuwa muzi (The mouth is responsible for discord among people). Indeed hatred induces a person to kill his/her neighbour. The biblical implication is that expressed in *James 3:5-10* concerning the danger of the "tongue" if it is not controlled.

2. Generosity/Kindness

Proverb: Kupaska nkhusunga (To give is to keep), also in Mnyako asani watufya mwembe mzimwiske (If your friend's beard catches fire, extinguish it). These two proverbs reveal how a person should behave to his/her fellow human being. The same concept is expressed in *2 Corinthians 9:7-8,* concerning stewardship. Also in *Acts of the Apostles 20:35.* "It is more blessed to give than to receive."

3. Justice and Friendship

Proverb: Cho chawona mnyako charuta mawa che paku iwe (What your friend has seen is gone, tomorrow it will see you). People should show concern for the misfortune of others. This is implied in the Bible as, "the same measure you give to others the same will be applied to you". The concept is expressed in *Matthew 7:1-5),* on judging others.

4. Good and evil

Proverb: Uheni uwele wakuwuchita (Evil returns to the doer). This is similar to what the book of Proverbs teaches. Evil people are trapped in their own sins, while honest people are happy and free (*Proverbs 29:6*).

5. The Providence of God

Proverb: Chiuta, mlerawana (God, the Nourisher). God is also the *Msunga* (The Keeper), and called *Mlimiliya* (Caretaker). All these ideas about God are found in the Bible. For instance, in *Genesis 22:8-14,* God is the Provider.

What the Gospel Corrects or Replaces

Despite the fact, clearly demonstrated above, that the Bible affirms many of the beliefs and values of the Tonga, it must be admitted that there are Tonga traditional beliefs, practices and values that biblical teaching does not support. In the light of Christ's teachings, these traditional values need to be corrected.

The following are a few examples

1. **Retaliation:** The Tonga say: **Jisu ku jisu** (An eye for an eye.) When someone has injured another, the judgement is held to be **jisu ku jisu.** Even though the Mosaic (Old Testament) law would seem to support this, Jesus did not support revenge. Instead, he taught that we should forgive those who offend us (Matthew 5:38-40). One is to forgive seventy times seven (Matthew 18:22); for if we do not forgive others, God will not forgive the wrongs we have done, but if we forgive them, our heavenly Father will also forgive us (Matthew 6:14-15).

Conclusion

The few examples cited above show that the Bible affirms in Tonga religious beliefs and values. The Bible also corrects and replaces some of the values. . It is in light of both the affirmations and corrections that the churches should set clear policies on the inculturation of the Word of God. As of now very little attention is paid to this important task.

4. Suggestions for Further Study and Reflection

A. Revaluing our Tonga Heritage

The introductory chapters of this work have shown the significance of the use of Tonga proverbs. The proverbs embody the Tonga traditional norms, values, philosophy, wisdom, beliefs and practices. In some cases they show the drive that motivates moral behaviour in young people. Therefore, my argument is that the representative proverbs collected in this book express behavioural attitudes, life experiences, social rules of conduct, traditional cultural values, common sense knowledge, codified wisdom, and truth of the Tonga people. Proverbs are not mere entertainments.

Unfortunately the early white missionaries who spread the Gospel in Tongaland did not encourage some of the Tonga positive customs. Some of the dances and songs which embody Tonga cultural heritage were condemned such as Malipenga, Chioda, Gule Wakawole, Mchoma, etc. Some of Tonga proverbs would be wrapped up in the songs and give meaning to the truth about people.

Donald Fraser illustrates this hatred of Tonga customs and rituals in the following quotation.

Often how I heard Dr. Elmslie speak of the awful customs of the Tonga and Tumbuka, but the actual sight of some of these gave a shock and horror that will leave one speechless. The atmosphere seems charged with vice. It is the only theme that runs through songs, and games, and dances. Here sure is the seat of Satan... You turn out to the village square to see the lads and girls at play. They are dancing; but every act is awful in its shamelessness and an old grandmother, bent and withered has entered the circle to incite the boys and girls to more loathsome dancing. You go back to your tent bowed with an awful shame, to hide yourself.... The next morning the village is gathered together to see your carriers at the worship, and to hear the news of the white stranger. You improve the occasion, and stand, ashamed to speak of what you saw. The same boys and girls are there, the same old grandmothers... and when you are gone, the same horror is practised under the same clear moon.[6]

The problem of the Tonga people still clinging to traditions in spite of the preaching of the Gospel was a common thing throughout Malawi and wherever the missionaries ventured. As a result Tonga oral literature was little used for contextualising the Gospel. This is why very little is written on Tonga oral literature. The Tonga oral literature was withdrawn from schools of Tongaland and replaced with Tumbuka and Chewa languages. This policy meant to kill the Tonga cultural heritage. The contemporary generation would lose their dialect. This also meant that the Tonga myths, folktales, proverbs and riddles were endangered.

The purpose of this book is to preserve some of the Tonga proverbs before they are completely eroded. The appeal is that the Church in Malawi should take good advantage of the African practice of using proverbs to explain, confirm or summarize a message. It has been indicated in Chapter Two how our Lord Jesus Christ used the proverbs from His cultural heritage to teach truths and moral lessons. The Old Testament devotes a full volume to proverbs, i.e., the "Book of Proverbs."

If we want the Gospel to spread and to become at home in Malawi, we could not hope for a better re-interpretation of the text. And the Gospel will not be at home in Malawi before it is on people's lips as proverb and song. Only when our language changes can our thinking change, and with it our belief system and our philosophy of life. The corpus of proverbs is our only literary thesaurus of didactic character. The exhortation function of the proverbs is closely connected with its conservation of survival in our oral tradition. I therefore urge preachers and teachers to make use of proverbs effectively in their respective situations.

---

[6] Source: *Life and Work*, No. 1881, April 1904, Livingstonia Mission, p. 6. Dr. Elmslie once worked as missionary in Tongaland.

B. Possible Objections to Using African Proverbs in the Church

For various reasons not all who read this book may like the idea of using proverbs for preaching the Word of God. Some readers may feel that since African proverbs are part of the African traditional culture, Christians must not go back to them. Other people may be reluctant to use African proverbs because of fear that they may overshadow the Bible message, since some of the proverbs are so clear that they may be more easily remembered than the Bible texts they are meant to explain. In certain cases some traditional proverbs may be contradictory to the teachings of the Bible. For example some Tonga proverbs say:

♦ Ulemu ubaya (Kindness can kill)

♦ Nkhondo ndi mnasi (The one who starts war is your neighbour)

♦ Lipambe likuryi (May the lightning eat you) etc.

The first proverb contradicts the Christian teaching to be kind to your neighbour. The second proverb contradicts the Christian exhortation to love your neighbour. The third proverb contradicts the Christian teaching against cursing your friend. Yet in traditional setting, these proverbs may have a positive meaning and explanation. Some proverbs may relate to the concept of ancestral veneration, which is rejected by some Christians.

C. Responses to the Objections

Obviously some of these objections to the use of indigenous African proverbs in the Church are quite strong. The question is, what do you yourself think of them? For our part, we think that there are responses to them that are equally strong and worthy of careful and sympathetic consideration. In the light of such objections should we endanger our proverbs? It does not mean that all aspects of African culture are heathen or unchristian. Culture is very broad. It includes, for example, the beliefs of a people, i.e., about God or the nature of humans; their values, i.e., what they regard as good or bad, right or wrong, and, therefore ought not to be done, or what they consider to be true or beautiful; their customs or folklore, i.e., how they behave, relate to others, talk, dress, their etiquette, etc; the institutions that help them to express the above, such as the social structure, the institution of chieftaincy, the family, system of government, courts, markets, clubs and associations.

All these systems of beliefs, values, customs, and institutions bind a people together and give them a sense of identity, dignity, security and continuity.

If some of the proverbs are contradictory to the truth of the Bible, the preacher should not build his/her sermon around such proverbs. The Bible itself should speak to the people. The proverbs should be used when the Gospel affirms them, as indicated in some of my suggestions. As noted earlier, some of the proverbs may not necessarily be used for Biblical explanation, but rather in certain traditional settings to warn and advise. This is why ethical values have a diversity. What is normally accepted in one society may not necessary be acceptable in another. In speaking about ancestral veneration other societies feel that they need to receive due respect because they are the custodians of morality. The moral principles were passed on from the "departed" or the "living-dead" to the living elders and thereby to the youth.

D. Advantages in Using Proverbs

The exhortative function of the proverb is closely connected with its survival in the oral tradition. The proverb is the last living genre in the oral traditions of urbanized, modernised people. Proverbs in a living non-urbanised community are the essential collection of moral precepts, from which no individual may deviate without risking the disapproval of his/her community. Proverbs serve as a window into worldview. It is because of these advantages and those noted earlier that our Lord Jesus Christ himself used proverbial sayings frequently. He succeeded in getting his hearers to understand and respond to his message even though some did not always accept it. The proverbs drew their attention and provoked their imaginations. Experience has shown that most of the preachers who use proverbs have sustained the interest and attention of their hearers.

E. Suggestions for Further Study and Follow-Up

This book is one of the series which have been published mainly for preachers and teachers as part of a wider project on the study of African proverbs. We would encourage scholars and educational institutions to find ways of keeping this effort going. We should not fall into the trap of endangering our proverbs. It will be a good idea if Theological Colleges, Seminaries and other Educational Institutions of African Studies undertake paremiology (proverb study) seriously and integrate this study into other disciplines, such as Theology, History, Languages, Geography, and so on.

Religious leaders should be keen to explore African proverbs as one aspect of inculturation of the Word of God. This contextualisation of the Word of God will make more sense to the indigenous people. I would like to urge young educated people from different ethnic groups in Malawi as well as Africa as a whole, that all of us should start collecting proverbs from our societies which are endangered. Composers and poets should frequently use proverbs on Radio, Video, and TV. The teachers should teach proverbs as part of their cultural studies, and during periods when moral and social values are taught.

For those who are interested to preserve their cultural heritage through proverbs, we suggest that the study may follow the pattern used in this book. Readers, especially teachers and preachers can collect proverbs in their own mother tongues and record them. They may write notes on those collected or those already in print. The notes may follow the pattern used in this book or some other style. Teachers can use a thematic approach, i.e., categorise proverbs into themes addressing obedience and disobedience; justice; cooperation; love; unity, etc. The proverbs should be critically analysed so as to discover what the Gospel affirms about their values, or adds, or corrects, or replaces, and what values and themes these address. Do they address ethical values of the society? Do they address some theological issues that are related to the Bible, etc?

In conclusion we must attempt to make Christianity (or any other world religion) part of the African's way of life. The missionaries completely ignored this ancient heritage of the African peoples even though this literary language of proverbs would have been the perfect medium for teaching the Bible. The question is, can we use African proverbs for the evangelisation of Africa? As an author of this book, I would like to confess that there is much one would need to explore in the use of proverbs. It is my hope that those talented poets, mother tongue speakers, preachers or teachers who will venture to explore more of this valuable task, will even do a better job than the work of this author.

PART II

THE PROVERBS

194 Annotated Tonga Proverbs for Preaching and Teaching

Annotation Style

In this part of the book, one hundred and ninety four Tonga Proverbs are presented. Each of them has notes written on it in six sections.

1. First, the common version of **the proverb in Tonga** is given.

2. English edition, a literal translation of the proverb is given in **English**.

3. Under **Explanation/Origin**, a literal explanation of the proverb is given. In a few cases, this section also gives the story of the origin of the proverb. In most cases, the origin is not known; in such cases, only the literal or primary meaning is given. Thus, the explanation is limited to the image used, the actual life situation depicted, custom or history referred to, etc.

4. Under **Meaning**, the deeper or real meaning and moral lesson of the proverb is given.

5. Then, under **Occasion for Citing the Proverb**, the actual or probable occasions on which the proverb is used in traditional society are stated. Also, the specific or possible purposes for which the proverb is cited are stated. Possible occasions or purposes for which the proverb can be used in Christian preaching and teaching are also suggested.

6. Finally, under the heading **Related Key Biblical Themes/Stories**, a number of Bible passages, themes, stories, etc. are cited. These are examples of texts, etc. which one can use the proverb to explain or emphasise.

Preachers and teachers are encouraged to use these proverbs either in the forms stated here, or in modified forms. The Bible texts, etc. can also be added to, but care should be taken to see that the proverbs used suit them.

1. A Chigulano

A sickly or needy person

Expl: The proverb depicts a person who is perpetually weak and sickly—that is, a disadvantaged, poor, or disabled person.

Meaning: A person who needs support in order to survive.

Occasion: Cited when talking about the poor, needy, marginalised or disadvantaged people in Tonga society who need some help. Preachers use the proverb to refer to the needy in spirit, who need the word of salvation. Christians are exhorted to help the needy around them.

Related Biblical Themes and Stories:
1) "Large crowds came to him, bringing with them the lame, the blind, the crippled, the dumb, and many other sick people whom they placed at Jesus' feet; and he healed them" *(Matthew 15:30)*.

2) "There at the Beautiful Gate, as it was called, was a man who had been lame all of his life" *(Acts 3:2-6)*. Peter and John healed him.

3) "A man was there who had been sick for thirty-eight years" *(John 5:5-6)*.

2. A matuwuyo

A person you don't know well

Expl: A person who is never trusted and carries unreliable information.

Meaning: An unpredictable person or a double-heart. Sometimes refers to a person believed to practice witchcraft.

Occasion: Cited when advising a person to be careful about his/her dealings with someone known to be unpredictable in his/her actions. Sometimes it refers to a person believed to be a witch, so people should be careful dealing with such a person.

Related Biblical Themes and Stories:
1) "Everyone utters lies to his neighbour; with flattering lips and a double heart they speak" *(Psalm 12:2 RSV)*.

2) "A person like that, unable to make up his mind and undecided in all he does, must not think that he will receive anything from the Lord" *(James 1:8).*

3) "Purify your hearts, you hypocrites!" *(James 4:8).*

3. Abaya Soro cha

You don't kill a honey-bird

Expl/Origin: There is a legend that the Tonga people call the honey-bird *Soro* because it has power to draw people after it and show them something important. In most cases it leads them to a beehive with plenty of honey.

Meaning: You should not reject or despise a virtuous person who is helping the people he/she influences.

Occasion for Citing the Proverb: The proverb is used when advising people to respect those who care for them in their families or community. That is, they should not be despised. Preachers have cited it to decry how the Jews killed Jesus, who was the source of their salvation.

Related Biblical Themes and Stories:

1) We would never leave the Lord to serve other gods! The Lord our God brought our fathers and us out of slavery in Egypt and we saw the miracles that he performed. He kept us safe wherever we went among all the nations through which we passed (Joshua 24:16-17).

2) Peter and John condemned the Jews for killing Jesus because He is the one of whom the scripture says, "The stone that you the builders despised turned out to be the most important of all". Salvation is to be found through him alone; in all the world there is no one else whom God has given who can save us *(Acts 4:11-12).*

4. Amunkhwele asekana viphata

Baboons laugh at each other's bare pads

Expl: People often talk about things that involve others and not those involving themselves.

Meaning: A person should mind his/her own business.

Occasion: The proverb is cited for those people who are hypocrites. They would like to condemn others, while they too are equally condemned. In other words, people should not despise others.

Related Biblical Themes and Stories:

1) David became very angry at the rich man and said, "I swear by the living Lord that the man who did this ought to die. For having done such a cruel thing he must pay back four times as much as he took." "You are that man." Nathan said to David. (*2 Samuel 12:5-7*).

2) You hypocrite! First take the log out of your own eye, and then you will see clearly to take the speck out of you brother's eye (*Matthew 7:5*).

5. Boza liwele mweneko

A lie returns to the one who tells it

Expl: Usually liars are exposed in the community.

Meaning: You should not tell lies about people in their absence, since such lies are bound to be exposed and thereby you will get ashamed of yourself.

Occasion: This proverb is usually cited in courts where the accused persons bear false witness to each other. It is used to advise someone to stop telling lies. Young people are warned against telling lies.

Related Biblical Themes and Stories:

1) One of the seven things that the Lord hates and cannot tolerate is "a witness who tells one lie after another" (*Proverbs 6:19*).

2) Isaiah deplored the people of Judah for depending on lies and deceit to keep them safe (*Isaiah 28:15*).

3) The Lord said that hailstorms would sweep away all the lies they depended on and floods would destroy their security (*Isaiah 28:17b*). That is, God will expose their lies and they will be humiliated.

4) In the story of Ananias and Sapphira, Peter exposed their lies and they were humiliated: Peter said to him, "Ananias, why did you let Satan take control of you and make you lie to the Holy Spirit by keeping part of the money you received for the property?" (*Acts 5:3*).

6. Changa epa wamko ku mchira wataya

If you hold a squirrel by the tail, you lose it

Expl: If one wants to catch a squirrel, avoid grabbing its tail. It easily slips away, leaving part of its tail behind.

Meaning: Certain things are short-lived, so one must be careful in making decisions.

Occasion: Used to warn a person against clinging to something which is short-lived. For instance, one should seek for a permanent job. The proverb is also cited when people want to deal with a culprit involved in a particular case, in order to catch him.

Related Biblical Themes and Stories:

1) "Do not store up riches for yourselves here on earth, where moths and rust destroy, and robbers break in and steal. Instead, store up riches for yourselves in heaven" (*Matthew 6:19-20).*

2) "Judas agreed to it and started looking for a good chance to hand Jesus over to them" (*Mark 14:11*).

7. Charu mbanthu

People are the world

Expl: The world cannot be enjoyable without people.

Meaning: A person should be careful with his/her life.

Occasion: Cited when advising young people not to be careless with their lives, because they are the source of the next generation. Sometimes it is used in times of epidemic, when many people are dying. Hence, it is a caution to those living to be extra careful, because they will make the world of tomorrow.

Related Biblical Themes and Stories:

1) "Does a person gain anything if he wins the whole world but loses his life?" (*Mark 8:36*).

2) "He was in the world, and the world was made through him, yet the world knew him not" (*John 1:10*).

3) "I have given them thy word, and the world has hated them because they are not of the world, even as I am not of the world" (*John 17:14* RSV).

8. Chifukwa chawezi waku Chiuta nyumba yazungula

Because of the grace of God the house (i.e., household) is satisfied

Expl: God is merciful, and because of his grace he gives the family what it needs.

Meaning: Through God's grace, the family will be happy.

Occasion: Cited when thanking God for his gifts; for example, having food in times of drought.

Related Biblical Themes and Stories:

1) "Bless me, God, and give me much land. Be with me and keep me from anything evil that might cause me pain" *(I Chronicles 4:10).*

2) "I will richly provide Zion with all she needs; I will satisfy her poor with food" *(Psalm 132:15).*

3) "Come back to the Lord your God. He is kind and full of mercy; he is patient and keeps his promise" *(Joel 2:13).*

4) "I knew that you are a loving and merciful God" *(Jonah 4:2).*

9. Chigau ndi ku mupozwa

A good harvest of cassava is determined by young growing cuttings

Expl: The society should take proper care of the youth. Also, the youth need to work hard to acquire the skills and knowledge employed in adult life. The Tonga look at the young cassava seedlings in forecasting a bumper yield. The proverb is metaphorically used.

Meaning: Today's youth are the future nation.

Occasion: Cited at funerals when a young person has died. The lesson is that through such deaths the society loses future leaders. Sometimes it is used in reproach for mistreating a young person, or when reprimanding a young person for his/her lack of knowledge. The youth are warned against indulging in habits which can bring them to early death; e.g., sex outside marriage.

Related Biblical Themes and Stories:

1) Never forget God's commandments, and teach them to your children (*Deuteronomy 6:6-7 and Psalm 78:5-7*).

2) The proverb can be related to Jesus' regard for the children. Jesus said, "Let the children come to me and do not stop them, because the Kingdom of God belongs to such as these" (*Luke 18:16*).

10. Chikumbu chimoza chituswa nyinda cha

One thumb cannot crush a louse

Expl: The problems requiring a people's collective efforts always exist. It is difficult for the one thumb to destroy a louse without the help of another thumb, just as it is equally difficult for one person to solve a problem. This is equivalent to "No man is an island."

Meaning: Unity is strength. We rely on each other or one another.

Occasion: This proverb is cited when advising young people on the need for unity in the house, the village, the community. Politicians use it when they campaign for their parties in order to win in elections. Preachers use the proverb to help people understand Church unity.

Related Biblical Themes and Stories:

1) In the history of Israel under Kings David and Solomon things were all right because the kingdom of Israel was united. It was not possible for the enemies to take over the kingdom. After the divided kingdom we see that in 721 BC the Northern kingdom was captured by the Assyrians, and later on in 586 BC Judah was captured by the Babylonians (*II Kings 17 and II Kings 25; also Isaiah 7-8:36-39*).

2) In *John 17*, Jesus prays for unity among his disciples. (*John 17:21-23*).

3) The unity of the Church functions like a human body: All of you are Christ's body, and each one is a part of it (*I Corinthians 12:12-31*).

11. Chingana nyoko wawi ndi nyivu ndi nyoko mbwenu

Even though your mother has gray hair, she is still your mother

Expl: Elderly parents with gray hair are sometimes despised. Young people should love their parents although they are getting old and may not appear attractive or firm.

Meaning: A person should not disown his/her parents just because they happen to be poor, of low social status or old.

Occasion: It is used when advising young people who exhibit such deplorable attitudes to their parents.

49

Related Biblical Themes and Stories:

1) The proverb addresses the theme of respect as reflected in the fifth commandment: "Respect you father and your mother, so that you may live a long time in the land that I am giving you" (*Exodus 20:12*).

2) A wise son makes his father proud of him; a foolish one brings his mother grief (*Proverb 10:1*).

3) When your mother is old, show her your appreciation (*Proverbs 23:22*).

4) Anyone who makes fun of his father or despises his mother in her old age ought to be eaten by vultures or have his eyes picked out by wild ravens (*Proverbs 30:17*).

12. Chinjeru chendi ndamwene

I have the wisdom, I can do it

Expl: A person who is self-conceited does not take other people's advice.

Meaning: It is dangerous to despise or neglect someone's advice.

Occasion: Cited when rebuking a person who has got into trouble after ignoring another's advice.

Related Biblical Themes and Stories:

1) "Stupid people have no respect for wisdom and refuse to learn" (*Proverbs 1:7*).

2) "People who are proud will soon be disgraced. It is wiser to be modest" (*Proverbs 11:2*).

3) "There is more hope for a stupid fool than for someone who speaks without thinking" (*Proverbs 29:20*).

13. Chipepe cheku Nyika; Ndi wondwe

There is heavy rain on the *Nyika*. It is spring

Expl: The opening words of a Tonga traditional rain prayer used by the Tonga when requesting rain to make their seeds grow. God is *Mlenga-Vuwa* (Rain Maker) in Tonga.

Meaning: In the heavens, there is an abundance of rain.

Occasion: Cited in a prayer for rain during a drought.

Related Biblical Themes and Stories:

1) "He sends rain on the land and he waters the fields" *(Job 5:10)*.

2) "You make springs flow in the valleys and rivers run between the hills" (Psalm 104:10).

3) "My word is like the snow and the rain that comes down from the sky to water the earth" (Isaiah 55:10).

14. Chisausau che kuchanya

The riverweeds are springing from above, i.e., heaven

Expl: The thought is of the long ropes or river plants, lilies, and dark weeds which during the heavy rains get washed downstream and out into the lakes.

Meaning: The gathering of rain clouds.

Occasion: Chanted to serve as the opening words of a rain prayer. It is usually cited when there is need to pray for rains during a drought. The people look up to God as the giver of the rain.

Related Biblical Themes and Stories:

1) The proverb can illustrate the occasion in which Elijah prayed for rain on Mount Carmel. In a little while the sky was covered with dark clouds, the wind began to blow, and a heavy rain began to fall *(I Kings 18:41-45)*.

2) "Whenever I hold back the rain ... if they pray to me and repent and turn away from the evil they have been doing, then I will hear them" *(II Chronicles 7:13-14)*.

15. Chiuta Mlimiliya ndi Mlera-wana

God, the keeper and nourisher

Expl: These are proverbial attributes given to God during traditional offerings or sacrifices.

Meaning: God is the true giver and keeper of life, and the First Cause of all good harvests in the field.

Occasion: Preachers use this proverb when thanking God for the gifts he gives to his people, such as good rains, good harvest, and the like.

Related Biblical Themes and Stories:

1) "I have provided all kinds of grain and all kinds of fruit for you to eat" *(Genesis 1:29).*

2) "You make the grass grow for the cattle and plants for man to use, so that he can grow his crops" *(Psalm 104:14).*

3) "He gives food to every living creature. His love is eternal" *(Psalm 136:25).*

16. Chiuta waku chanya

The God of heaven

Expl: The Tonga believe that no person has seen God, and therefore, there is none to whom he may be compared, and there are no words with which to tell what he is like.

Meaning: God is invisible and sovereign.

Occasion: Preachers cite the proverb to show that the dwelling place of God is heaven, but that he is also the creator of the world (*Mlenga-charu*), the self-existent to whom worship should be offered. No man has seen this God (*Chauta/Chiuta*) who is invisible and eternal.

Related Biblical Themes and Stories:

1) "How clearly the sky reveals God's glory" *(Psalm 19:1).*

2) "To whom can the holy God be compared. Is there anyone else like him?" *(Isaiah 40:25).*

3) "Do you not know that I am everywhere in heaven and on earth?" *(Jeremiah 23:24)*

17. Chiuta wamto

God has taken him/her

Expl: This expresses the belief that death originates from God or that God wills that one should die and live with Him.

Meaning: A person receives life from God (Chiuta). Therefore, death is the call of Chiuta (God) who will take care of the dead.

Occasion: Cited during a funeral, to give hope and courage to the bereaved that the relative who is dead is the child of God who has called him/her to himself, and God will take care of him/her. It is also used in preaching to refer to God as the Creator, who takes back life to himself.

Related Biblical Themes and Stories:

1) "Moses, the Lord's servant died there in the land of Moab as the Lord had said he would. The Lord buried him in a valley in Moab, opposite the town of Bethpeor, but to this day no one knows the exact place of his burial" (*Deuteronomy 34:5-6*).

2) "God will take care of me" (*Psalm 27:10*).

3) "But God will rescue me; he will save me from the power of death" (*Psalm 49:15*).

18. Chiwele vuli chingubaya Tungwa

Returning killed the antelope

Expl: There is a folktale in Tonga oral literature where Antelope had to go back, postponing his journey. On his way back, he met Leopard who killed him.

Meaning: A person should be steady in making decisions. In other words, a decision passed should be adhered to.

Occasion: The proverb is cited to warn people against making hurried decisions, only to find that in the end they have messed up things. People should live by principles.

Related Biblical Themes and Stories:

"But Lot's wife looked back and was turned into a pillar of salt" (*Genesis 19:26*).

19. Chiyunisonganya

A double dealer

Expl: The proverb originates from a Tonga tale which tells of a bird named *Chiyuni-songany* which stirred up people from two villages to be enemies.

Meaning: A person who brings confusion to others.

Occasion: Cited to ridicule a person who is thought to be a busybody. Sometimes it is used to warn a person against associating with one who is a double dealer. Preachers use it to warn Christians against associating with liars.

Related Biblical Themes and Stories:

1) "The Lord hates and cannot tolerate a man who stirs up trouble among friends" *(Proverbs 6:19).*

2) "People with quick tempers cause a lot of quarreling and trouble" *(Proverbs 29:22).*

3) The story of Demetrius, who confused the crowd and caused the whole meeting to end in an uproar which spread throughout the whole city *(Acts 19: 21-34).*

20. Chizimbu chakubisamamo

A nest for hiding

Expl: The Tonga sometimes analogically use the word *chizimbu* (nest) to mean a house. Though not necessarily durable, it provides enough security to the owner.

Meaning: A house to live in.

Occasion: Cited to show appreciation for one's effort to own a house, which provides security and comfort.

Related Biblical Themes and Stories:

1) "Jesus said to him: 'Foxes have holes and birds have nests, but the Son of Man has no place to lie down and rest'" *(Luke 9:58).*

2) "Even the sparrows have built a nest, and the swallows have their home" *(Psalm 84:3).*

3) "A man away from home is like a bird away from its nest" *(Proverbs 27:8).*

21. Cho chingukwezga Pusi, chingukwezga Munkhwere

What made the monkey climb up a tree also made the baboon climb up

Expl: A person should not rejoice when others are ill-treated.

Meaning: It is unwise for a person to laugh at a colleague or a relative in difficulty, since he too may one day experience a similar situation.

Occasion: Used to advise a person to sympathise with or even help someone involved in a problem rather than rejoice over it. The teaching is worth noting by people in various walks of life, e.g., classmates who may see one of their members mistreated by their teacher, workers who may see some colleagues unfairly dealt with by a cruel master, or even citizens who may see the rights of some fellow nationals infringed upon by a dictatorial leader. It is also used to warn young people against neglecting their peers who fall into trouble.

Related Biblical Themes and Stories:

1) "You are my friends! Take pity on me! The hand of God has struck me down" (*Job 19:21*).

2) "Let not those rejoice over me who are wrongfully my foes, and let not those wink the eye who hate me without cause" (*Psalm 35:19* RSV).

3) "Don't be glad when your enemy meets disaster, and don't rejoice when he stumbles. The Lord will know if you are gloating and he will not like it, and then maybe he won't punish him" (*Proverbs 24:17-18*).

22. Cho chituza chitumba ng'oma cha

A thing that comes does not beat a drum

Expl: Certain things come to us by surprise; therefore, we should always be ready.

Meaning: An urgent thing must be given prompt attention.

Occasion: Used when advising a person to attend to a problem promptly in order to prevent it from worsening. Sometimes in a job situation, young people are advised to complete their tasks for they do not know when the boss will need the final report. In order to safeguard the job, one needs to complete the task in good time. Also, a watchman is warned not to sleep in the night, lest thieves rob the property he guards.

Related Biblical Themes and Stories:

1) "I lie awake; I am like a lonely bird on a housetop" (*Psalm 102:7*).

2) "I will climb my watchtower and wait to see what the Lord will tell me to say and what answer he will give to my complaint" (*Habakkuk 2:1*).

3) "Keep watch and pray that you will not fall into temptation" (*Matthew 26:41*).

4) Our Lord Jesus Christ constantly warned his hearers to keep watch. "Watch then because you do not know when the master of the house is coming—it might be in the evening or midnight or before dawn or at sunrise. If he comes suddenly, he must not find you asleep. What I say to you then I say to all: 'Watch!'" (*Mark 13:35-36*).

5) "The end of all things is near. You must be self-controlled and alert, to be able to pray" (*I Peter 4:7*).

23. Cho chiwengi pano nchakutose

Whatever happens here, happens to us all

Expl: We should not rejoice at the misfortune of a neighbour. In a community we should learn to solve problems together.

Meaning: What your neighbour has seen is gone; tomorrow it will see you.

Occasion: Cited when encouraging people to live out the values of cooperation and inter-dependence. It is also a warning to people against committing some evil which can bring suffering upon innocent people.

Related Biblical Themes and Stories:

1) The story of Achan's sin: the people of Israel suffered innocently. It was not until Joshua had discovered the culprit that things were made better. Achan was seized. Joshua said, "Why have you brought such troubles on us? The Lord will now bring trouble to you today" *(Joshua 7:25).*

2) "The sailors said to each other, 'Let's draw lots and find out who is to blame for getting us into this danger'. They did so, and Jonah's name was drawn" *(Jonah 1:7-8).* Thus the sin of Jonah brought trouble to all who were in this ship.

24. Cho untanja ndichu chipunduwa

A habit that you like could destroy you

Expl: A person should not over-indulge in silly habits.

Meaning: Excessive indulgence in a thing is harmful.

Occasion: Used when advising some people who do not control their bad behaviour, e.g., drinking, fighting, smoking.

Related Biblical Themes and Stories:

1) Don't spend all your energy on sex and all your money on women; they have destroyed kings (*Proverbs 31:3*).

2) Jesus warned those who had sinned but had been forgiven, lest something worse would happen to them (*John 5:13*).

25. Chuma chiwe cha pa nyifwa, kweni pa umoyo pe

Bridewealth never goes back at death

Expl: The proverb reflects marriage customs. The Tonga say that in the olden days, a husband always had wealth (*chuma*) or "a big case" when his wife died—whether the union was formal or informal. The payment he had to make to his wife's people was called *chisoka*. Sometimes land was given instead of money.

Meaning: Bridewealth is never returned to the husband or his kin group on the death of his wife.

Occasion: Cited at the death of a husband or a wife. The value of the money is considerable, especially at the death of a wife. When the relatives are satisfied, they would give permission to bury the body or else delay the burial until the payment is effected.

Related Biblical Themes and Stories:

1) "I am a foreigner living here among you, sell me some land so that I can bury my wife" *(Genesis 23:4).*

26. Garu yiruma mbuyake

A dog bites its master

Expl: A hungry dog, if provoked, can bite even its master.

Meaning: A person should be careful the way he/she handles things.

Occasion: Used when warning people who are careless with their lives to take heed whatever they do. Sometimes it is used as a warning against being self-conceited or proud.

Related Biblical Themes and Stories:

1) The Israelites turned against their God and made him angry: "When Israel was a child, I loved him and called him out of Egypt as my son. But the more I called to him, the more he turned away from me" (*Hosea 11:1-2*).

2) "God resists the proud but shows favour to the humble" (*Proverbs 3:34; I Peter 5:5*).

27. Ine nde munthukazi ndi munthurume

I am the woman and the man

Expl: In Tonga, the proverb refers to a person who sees himself or herself as a key representative.

Meaning: I can represent both husband and wife.

Occasion: Commonly cited by the one who represents both husband and wife during an arbitration to settle a dispute in a marriage. Such a person has the authority to accept the decisions made on behalf of both husband and wife. Preachers can use the proverb to show the position of Jesus as the representative of both God and humans.

Related Biblical Themes and Stories:

1) "But to all who receive him, who believed in his name, he gave power to become children of God" (*John 1:12* RSV).

2) "Therefore he is the mediator of a new covenant, so that those who are called may receive the promised eternal inheritance" (Hebrews 9:15).

3) "I am writing this to you, my children, so that you will not sin; but if anyone does sin, we have someone who pleads with the Father on our behalf—Jesus Christ, the righteous one" (I John 2:1).

28. Ise te pakatikati

We stand in the middle

Expl: This proverb is frequently used as a metaphor. The speaker sees himself/herself as a genealogical center where many kinship ties converge.

Meaning: A person who holds a central position in the genealogy of kinship ties.

Occasion: Often cited in discussions which follow the death of a relative. It is a proverb that is used to look down upon those who are helpless. Preachers use it to tell Christians that Jesus holds the key position for their salvation.

Related Biblical Themes and Stories:

1) "This is my blood, which seals God's covenant, my blood poured out for many for the forgiveness of sins" *(Matthew 26:28).*

2) "The very stone which the builders rejected has become the head of the corner" *(Mark 12:10; Psalm 118:22-23* RSV*).*

3) "The Lord God will give him the throne of his father David and he will reign over the house of Jacob for ever" *(Luke 1: 32-33* RSV*).*

29. Jenda-yija wangukukurwa ndi maji

A lone traveler was swept away by a stream

Expl: The proverb is based on Tonga legends that lone travelers have disappeared without any trace. It was common for Tonga people in the old days to travel to South Africa alone and never return. It was thought that either wild beasts which were prevalent at the time or slave traders had captured them. The equivalent English proverb is: "Two is company, one is none."

Meaning: There is danger in travelling alone. We need to have fellowship with other people.

Occasion: Related to the theme of having fellowship with others, it is used to remind travelers of the importance of company for security. It can also be used particularly to warn urban dwellers who walk at night to beer parties or for other purposes. Young people should choose good company in which they can share good moral habits.

Related Biblical Themes and Stories:

1) "Enoch walked with God" *(Genesis 5:22-23).* He spent his life in fellowship with God who protected his life.

2) "Two are better than one, because together they can work more effectively. If one of them falls down the other can help him up. But if someone is alone and falls, it is just too bad because there is no one to help him" *(Ecclesiastes 4:9-12).*

3) Jesus sent two of his disciples ahead to find a colt in a village in Bethany (*Mark 11:1-2*). This was to ensure that there was security between them.

30. Juwani lapa mchenga nkhwambiya pamoza

If you want to win a race on sand, you should start at once

Expl: Part of Tonga land is along the lakeside, and its beautiful beaches have heaps of sand. It is difficult to walk on sand and even more difficult to race on sand.

Meaning: It is better to start your work early so that it can bring good results.

Occasion: Cited to advise young people to be vigilant, diligent, and hard working, especially those who are at school. They are advised to work hard from their earliest classes, since knowledge accumulates. Pupils trained in running races are advised not to look behind when they compete with others. Farmers are advised to clear their lands early so that they may have better harvests.

Related Biblical Themes and Stories:

1) "It comes out in the morning like a happy bridegroom, like an athlete eager to run a race" (*Psalm 19:5, TEV*).

2) "Jeremiah, if you get tired racing against men how can you race against horses?" (*Jeremiah 12:5*).

3) "Surely you know that runners take part in a race but only one of them wins the prize. Run then, in such a way as to win the prize. Every athlete in training submits to strict discipline in order to be crowned with a wreath that will not last; but we do it for one that will last forever. That is why I run straight for the finishing-line" (*I Corinthians 9:24-27*).

4) "As for us, we have this large crowd of witnesses around us. So then, let us rid ourselves of everything that gets in the way, and of the sin which holds on to us so tightly, and let us run with determination the race that lies before us" (*Hebrews 12:1*).

31. Kajipempheri wanguweku ku Marambo, Virizanga wangwachifwa

A beggar came back with wealth from *Marambo*, the lazy one did not come back with nothing

Expl: *Marambo* was the old Tonga name for Zambia. Since the Tonga people have been adventurous, some went out to several countries in East, Central, and South Africa, looking for work. Those who worked hard came back home as rich people. The lazy ones died there because of hunger. The picture brought out in the proverb is that of a person who "worked" at least by begging. The one who simply sat down without even taking the initiative to beg, died. Thus, a person should take initiative in order to get something for his/her living.

Meaning: All good things are the result of effort.

Occasion: Used when advising people who seem to be destitute because of laziness to work in order to improve their condition. Pastors can use it to urge Christians to use the power that God gives them to their own good.

Related Biblical Themes and Stories:

1) "For everyone who asks receives, and he who seeks finds, and to him who knocks it will be opened" *(Matthew 7:8* RSV*)*.

2) "But much more in my absence work out your salvation with fear and trembling for God is at work in you" *(Philippians 2:12-13)*.

32. Kakuza kija kalaula

Nothing comes without working for it

Expl: A person should take the initiative to earn a living; things cannot come like manna from heaven.

Meaning: If you want something, you have to make an effort.

Occasion: Used when advising people who are idle and expect good things to come their way: one must move around in order to get them. Especially the lazy ones are warned against roaming about without taking initiative to find something for them to earn a living.

Related Biblical Themes and Stories:

1) "Cursed is the ground because of you, in toil you shall eat of it all the days of your life" (*Genesis 3:17*).

2) "When Jacob learned that there was grain in Egypt, he said to his sons, 'Why do you look at one another?' And he said, 'Behold, I have heard that there is grain in Egypt; go down and buy grain for us there that we may live and not die'" (*Genesis 42:1-2* RSV).

3) "See, the place where we dwell under your charge is too small for us. Let us go to the Jordan and each of us get there a log and let us make a place for us to dwell there" (*II Kings 6:1-2*).

33. Kakuza kija kasikuwa/kalaura

That which comes without work is a curse

Expl: The proverb is based on a Tonga principle that you cannot have something good without sweating for it.

Meaning: Nothing good can come without working for it.

Occasion: Told when advising young people to work hard in their fields in order to have abundant food. Students are advised to work hard at school so that they can pass their examinations and prepare themselves for a bright future.

Related Biblical Themes and Stories:

1) The proverb is related to the story of the "Fall of Man" in Genesis chapter 3. God said, "You will have to work hard and sweat to make the soil produce anything, until you go back to the soil from which you were formed" (*Genesis 3:19*).

2) "He will reward each one according to his deeds (*Matthew 16:27*).

34. Kana kaku Chiuta

A little child of God

Expl: This saying refers to a man who may sometimes be spoken of as a child of God or a child of the Wonderful or Wonder-Worker.

Meaning: A person is believed to be a child of God who does something beyond what a neighbour can do.

Occasion: Preachers use the proverb to refer to the baby Jesus as the Son of God. Sometimes it is used to refer to a person who lives a good, exemplary life in the community as a role model. Such is a child of God.

Related Biblical Themes and Stories:

1) "Then he took a child and had him stand in front of them. He put his arms around him" *(Mark 9:35)*.

2) "Whoever does not receive the Kingdom of God like a child will never enter it" *(Mark 10:15)*.

3) "For to us a child is born, to us a son is given" *(Isaiah 9:6 RSV)*.

35. Kanda apa nani ndi kandepo

Where you step I shall also step there

Expl: The proverb shows how true friendship should be. Friends should be kind to each other. The equivalent English proverb is, "A David and Jonathan."

Meaning: People who are great friends.

Occasion: Cited when referring to young people whose friendship appears so bound up that no one can separate them. Preachers often use the story of the friendship between David and Jonathan as a role model for cultivating true friendship.

Related Biblical Themes and Stories:

1) Jonathan swore eternal friendship with David because of his deep affection for him. He took off the robe he was wearing and gave it to David, together with his armour and also his sword, bow and belt *(I Samuel 18:3-4)*. Both David and Jonathan were crying as they kissed each other *(I Samuel 20:41)*.

2) Jesus said that the greatest love a person can have for his friends is to give his life for them *(John 15:13-14)*.

36. Kanje nkhamana kweni mukati mwake mwe mtima wa muti ukuru

Inside a small seed is hidden the pith of a large tree

Expl: There are certain things which look small but are of great importance.

Meaning: A person who is despised can become a leader or helper.

Occasion: Used to warn people against underrating others, just because they are weak. One day such people may be of great use to the community. Some can become leaders.

Related Biblical Themes and Stories:

1) "A man may rise from poverty to become king of his country or go from prison to the throne" *(Ecclesiastes 4:13)*.

2) "The kingdom of heaven is like a grain of mustard seed which a man took and sowed in his field; it is the smallest of all seeds, but when it has grown it is the greatest of shrubs and becomes a tree so that the birds of the air come and make nests in its branches" *(Matthew 13:31-32 RSV)*.

37. Kankhunguni aka katiyungwisa

A bedbug's sting has brought trouble to us

Expl: The analogy is to show that one is not at peace if faced by a problem, just as it is difficult to have a sound sleep in a house infested by bedbugs.

Meaning: A person becomes restless when he/she has carelessly handled an issue or when he/she is in trouble.

Occasion: Used to warn people to be careful when dealing with a problem. Sometimes it is used to ridicule those who rejoice over another's sufferings and who later on experience the same things.

Related Biblical Themes and Stories:

1) The story of the chief priests and Pharisees who became restless at the words of Jesus that he would be raised to life after three days. They found means of guarding the tomb, fearing the disciples might steal his dead body, and this last lie would be even worse than the first one *(Matthew 27:62-64)*. Yet Jesus was raised from death all the same.

2) The members of the Council became disturbed at the preaching of the Apostles. Gamaliel said, "Be careful with these men. You could find yourself fighting against God" *(Acts 5:33-40)*.

38. Kanthu kekose kendi nyengo yaki

Everything has its own time

Expl: Things happen according to their own time.

Meaning: A person should not force something to happen.

Occasion: Cited to advise people to wait patiently for some expected thing to happen at the right time. In other words, people are warned against being too anxious over things. Preachers constantly use this to refer to specific events in the society (e.g., sudden deaths and disasters caused by floods, etc.), and thereby console people.

Related Biblical Themes and Stories:

1) "For everything there is a season, and a time for every matter under heaven" (*Ecclesiastes 3:1*).

2) "The time is coming when I will make a new covenant with the people of Israel and with the people of Judah" (*Jeremiah 31:31-34*).

3) "Put it in writing because it is not yet time for it to come true. But the time is coming quickly, and what I show you will come true. It may seem slow in coming, but wait for it; it will not be delayed" (*Habakkuk 2:3*).

4) "But the time is coming and is already here, when by the power of God's Spirit people will worship the Father as he really is, offering him the true worship he wants" (*John 4:23*).

39. Kanthu nkhako kamunyako ndi nkhusku

A thing that is yours is yours, what belongs to your neighbour is only additional

Expl: You can do anything with a thing that belongs to you, but you cannot have authority over a thing that is not yours.

Meaning: A person has authority over something that belongs to him/her.

Occasion: Used when advising a person to be responsible and self-reliant. Young people should not always be dependent on other people's things, because if that thing gets damaged, they are likely to pay for it. Preachers cite the proverb when warning the people against being careless with life, because it belongs to God. No one has authority over one's own life.

Related Biblical Themes and Stories:

1) One of Elisha's men was disturbed to see that he lost an axe which did not belong to him: "What shall I do, sir?" he exclaimed to Elisha. "It was a borrowed axe!" *(II Kings 6:5)*.

2) "The man who used to rob must stop robbing and start working in order to earn a living for himself and be able to help the poor" (Ephesians 4:28)

40. Kanthu nkhamabuchi-buchi mumanja muwengi mwakusambasamba

Keep your hands ever clean, for things come unexpectedly

Expl: We should be prepared to withstand any unexpected event. It is like the Scout motto: "Be prepared".

Meaning: A person should be ready for any unpredictable event.

Occasion: Cited when advising a person to prepare his/her life for a bright future. Preachers have used it to advise Christians to keep watch, lest they are taken away by the devil. They are exhorted to live a faithful Christian life, for they do not know when death will come to them.

Related Biblical Themes and Stories:

1) "No one knows, however, when that day or hour will come—neither the angels in heaven, nor the Son; only the Father knows. Be on watch, be alert, for you do not know when the time will come" *(Mark 13:32)*.

2) "So then, we should not be sleeping like the others; we should be awake and sober" *(I Thessalonians 5:6)*.

41. Katundu wakuyeleka-yeleka ndiyo wafyo

A pile of little things is what makes a load heavy

Expl: The proverb originates from a legendary incident in which a humpback got his back stretched because of carrying a pile of heavy things on his back. The heavy weight of the load was what stretched his back.

Meaning: A person who postpones work every time is bound to find himself/herself not accomplishing the task as scheduled.

Occasion: Used to advise students to promptly attend to their studies or assignments given by their teachers. Preachers cite the proverb to warn people against indulging themselves in several bad habits which will make it difficult for them to live good Christian lives.

Related Biblical Themes and Stories:

1) "Catch the foxes, the little foxes, before they ruin our vineyard in bloom" *(Song of Solomon 2:15).*

2) "Come to me, all of you who are tired from carrying heavy loads, and I will give you rest" *(Matthew 11:28).*

Proverb 41: Katundu wakuyeleka-yeleka ndiyo wafyo
(A pile of little things is what makes a load heavy)

42. Kayuni epa kaja pa uta kalasika cha

A bird on your bow cannot be killed

Expl: A person seeks the assistance of another person when he/she is in difficulty. The equivalent English proverb is, "Blood is thicker than water." In Tonga society parents cannot decide on matters of marriage engagement of their daughter. It is the aunt who handles such issues.

Meaning: It is not easy for a judge to pass judgment against a relative.

Occasion: The setting of the proverb is at a court or at the elders' council, when a person objects to having his case tried by someone related to the other party in the conflict; or when a judge declines to settle a case involving a relative. Sometimes it is used to show one's failure to solve a problem which involves one directly, as in the case of a medicine man failing to cure himself. It is also used to advise children to ask others to help them when they are in trouble.

Related Biblical Themes and Stories:
1) "Doctor, heal yourself.' You will also tell me to do here in my hometown the same things you heard were done in Capernaum" (*Luke 4:23*).

43. Ko kwafwa Njovu kusowa cha

The news about the death of an elephant is widely spread

Expl: The elephant is the biggest land animal in the world, and its death can be known throughout the community. Thus, the proverb is used as an analogy to how quickly news related to an important person spreads.

Meaning: The death of an important person is widely known; or, something bad done by an important person will be known very quickly.

Occasion: Used to refer to matters related to a very popular person. It could be death or a hidden matter that comes into the open about that person. It is also used to advise those who hold key positions in society to behave well.

Related Biblical Themes and Stories:
1) It can be affirmed in the story of the two people going to Emmaus and on the way were discussing the death of Jesus, since it was known all over Jerusalem. They asked the "stranger": "Are you the only visitor in Jerusalem who does not know things that have been happening there these last few days?" (*Luke 24:13-24*).

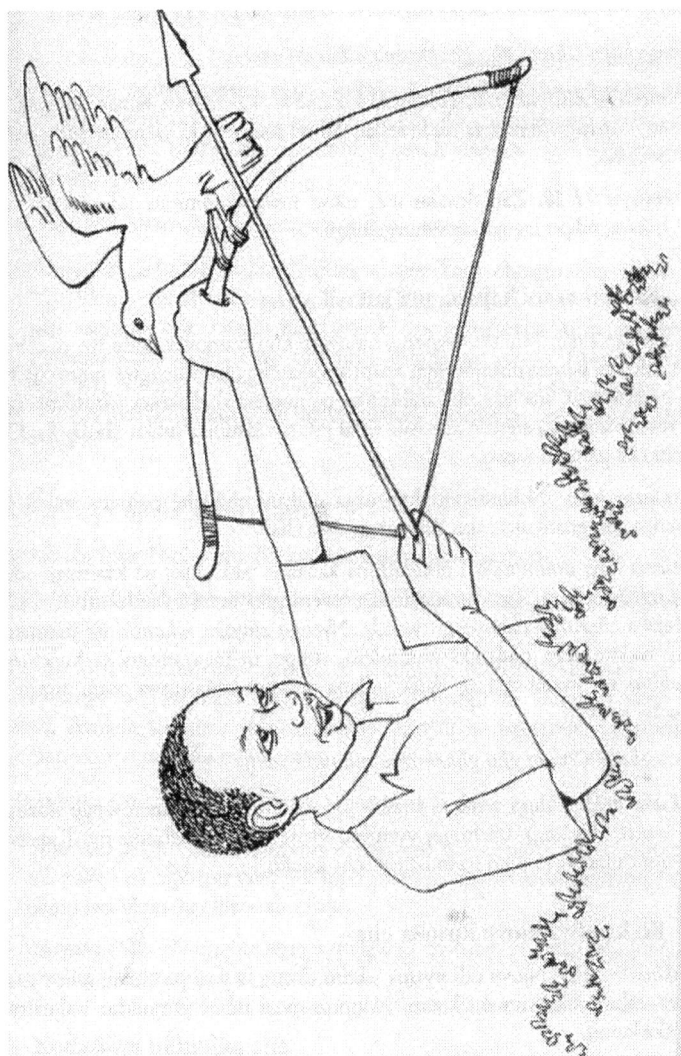

Proverb 42: Kayuni epa kaja pa uta kalasika cha
(A bird on your bow cannot be killed)

44. Kubaya njoka nkhu mutu

To kill a snake is to crush it on the head

Expl: A snake is easily killed if you crush its head.

Meaning: A person should handle a problem carefully.

Occasion: Used when advising young people who cannot solve the problems they meet in life to seek advice from the elders before they actually handle the problem.

Related Biblical Themes and Stories:

1) I will make you and the woman hate each other; her offspring and yours will always be enemies. Her offspring will crush your head" *(Genesis 3:15*

2) Do what your father tells you, my son, and never forget what your mother taught you" (Proverbs 6:20).

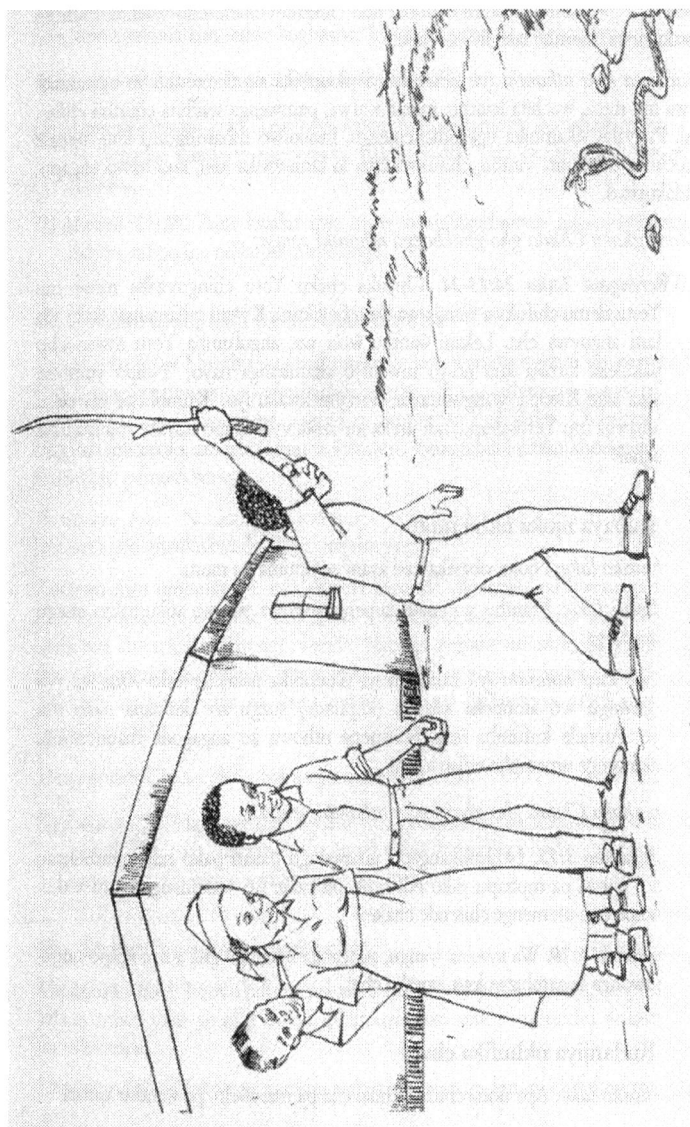

Poverb 44: Kubaya njoka nku mutu
(To kill a snake is to crush it on the head)

45. Kudanjiya nkhufika cha

Beginning does not mean ending

Expl: This imagery is drawn from a race. Starting early does not necessarily mean victory. People should be modest and industrious instead of being proud and boastful. The English equivalent is, "Pride goes before a fall."

Meaning: A person should not be boastful or proud of his/her plans but of his/her achievements.

Occasion: Cited to show disapproval for those who are boastful of their plans, but who do scarcely anything to implement them.

Related Biblical Themes and Stories:

1) "Whoever wants to be first must place himself last of all" *(Mark 9:35).*

2) "But many who now are first will be last and many who now are last will be first" *(Mark 10:31).*

3) "Surely you know that many runners take part in a race, but only one of them wins the prize" *(I Corinthians 9:24).*

46. Kufumba nkhuwona nthowa

To ask is the desire to know the way

Expl: There is no need to be self-conceited when in actual fact you know very little.

Meaning: It is always helpful to ask for advice before one does things that one is not sure about.

Occasion: Cited when reproaching a person who has made a serious mistake or has done something wrong because of his failure to seek advice in the first place. Pupils in a school setting should ask their teachers to show them how to do things correctly.

Related Biblical Themes and Stories:

1) "Ask, and you will receive, seek, and you will find; knock, and the door will be opened to you" *(Matthew 7:7).*

2) "The gate to life is narrow and the way that leads to it is hard and there are few people who find it" *(Matthew 7:14).*

3) "Thomas said to him, 'Lord we do not know where you are going; so how can we know the way?' Jesus answered him, 'I am the way, the truth, and the life; no one goes to the Father except by me'" (*John 14:5-6*).

47. Kufunyiya mata pasi

To spit on the ground

Expl: The proverb originates from a tale which tells how Hare obtained mercy from Elephant.

Meaning: To ask for mercy.

Occasion: Cited when a person pleads for help from someone. Sometimes it is used to plead for forgiveness for an offense one has committed against another person.

Related Biblical Themes and Stories:

1) "The servant fell on his knees before the King. 'Be patient with me,' he begged, 'and I will pay everything!' The King felt sorry for him, so he forgave him the debt and let him go" *(Matthew 18:26-27)*.

2) "Father Abraham! Take pity on me, and send Lazarus to dip his finger in some water and cool my tongue" *(Luke 16:24)*.

3) "And there was a widow in that same town who kept coming to him and pleading for her rights saying, 'Help me against my opponent'" *(Luke 18:3)*.

48. Kufwa ndi luzu

To die from thirst

Expl: The proverb originates from a Tonga legend according to which many people were believed to have died on their way to South Africa because of lack of water on the way.

Meaning: Water is important to keep a person alive.

Occasion: The proverb is cited when there is drought in the land, which is causing domestic animals to die.

Related Biblical Themes and Stories:

1) "He said to her, 'Please give me a drink of water; I am thirsty'" *(Judges 4:19).*

2) "They were hungry and thirsty and had given up all hope" *(Psalm 107:5).*

3) "I was hungry and you fed me, thirsty and you gave me a drink" *(Matthew 25:35).*

4) "Jesus said, 'I am thirsty'" *(John 19:28).*

49. Kuja umoyo wakuchigwangwala

To behave like *Chigwangwala* (a rat)

Expl: Chigwangwala is a showy small rat. When it meets its enemy, it stands erect, pretending to attack its enemy, then darts away very quickly. The analogy shows that there are people who pretend to behave in a way which is not their normal way of behaviour.

Meaning: A person who is proud and showy.

Occasion: Used to warn people against showing off. Such showy people have nothing or very little to contribute to society. Preachers use it to condemn people who are proud and deliberately live in sin.

Related Biblical Themes and Stories:

1) The horror you inspire has deceived you, and the pride of your heart, you who live in the clefts of the rock, who hold the height of the hill. though you make your nest as high a the eagle's I will bring you down from there, says the Lord "(*Jeremiah* 49:16 RVS)

2) "For everyone who makes himself great will be humbled, and everyone who humbles himself will be made great" (Luke 18:14).

50. Kujikama, uryengi kanthu ndi wala, kusoka uwengi waka

Kneeling you eat with elders, keep standing and you eat nothing

Expl: According to traditional etiquette, young people kneel in order to show respect to their elders.

Meaning: You learn a lot from elders when you are humble, but not when you are rude.

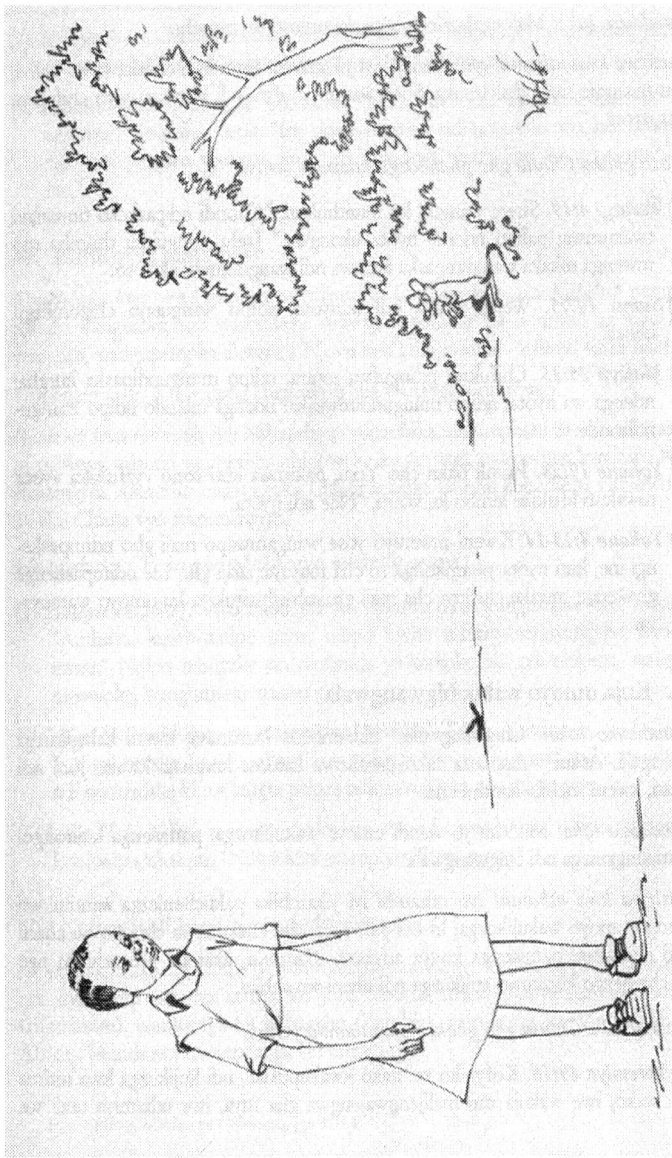

Proverb 49: Kuja umoyo waku chigwangwala
(To behave like chingwangwala)

Proverb 50: Kujikama, uryengi kanthu ndi wala, kusoka uwengi waka
(Kneeling you eat with elders, keep standing and you eat nothing)

Occasion: Cited when advising a young person to be good to elders in order to win their love and hence open to him/her their storehouse of knowledge and wisdom. Sometimes humble young people in the society are used as role models, because of their large amount of wisdom or wealth for their age. Those who have a stupid outlook are examples of those who have displayed bad behaviour to the elders.

Related Biblical Themes and Stories:

1) "It is better to be humble and stay poor than to be one of the arrogant and get a share of their loot" (*Proverbs 16:19*).

2 "I have sinned against God and against you. I am no longer fit to be called your son" (*Luke 15:21*).

3) God exalted Jesus because he was humble (*Philippians 2:11*). "And all will openly proclaim that Jesus Christ is Lord, to the glory of God the Father."

51. Kukana kwa mutu wa garu

To refuse like a dog's head

Expl: A dog's head is very hard to break even if it is run over by a vehicle. The proverb is used metaphorically.

Meaning: A person who is hardhearted or who has no sympathy for others.

Occasion: Used to reprimand a person who is hardhearted or a person who shows no sympathy for others. Sometimes it is used to caution young people who refuse to go on errands for elderly people.

Meaning: A person should not provoke situations because she/he happens to be in a group, since she/he may end up facing the consequences of his/her actions alone.

Occasion: Cited to warn the people against deliberately provoking a situation. Especially it warns people on the dangers of mob action.

Related Biblical Themes and Stories:

1) "They provoked the Lord to anger with their doings, and a plague broke out among them" (*Psalm 106:29* RSV).

2) "As he went away from there, the scribes and the Pharisees began to press him hard and to provoke him to speak of many things, lying in

Proverb 50: Kujikama, uryengi kanthu ndi wala, kusoka uwengi waka wait for him, to catch him at something he might say" (*Luke 11:53-54* RSV).

3) "When the people of Israel provoked the Lord in the wilderness for forty years, they perished" (*Hebrews 3:17*).

52. Kukanda pa moto

To step on fire.

Expl: People should examine their positions carefully before involving themselves in incidents that may have serious consequences. Equivalent to the English proverb, "Let sleeping dogs lie."

Meaning: A person should not provoke situations because she/he happens to be in a group, since she/he may end up facing the consequences of his/her actions alone.

Occasion: Cited to warn the people against deliberately provoking a situation. Especially it warns people on the dangers of mob action.

Related Biblical Themes and Stories:
1) "They provoked the Lord to anger with their doings, and a plague broke out among them" (*Psalm 106:29* RSV).

2) "As he went away from there, the scribes and the Pharisees began to press him hard and to provoke him to speak of many things, lying in wait for him, to catch at something he might say" (*Luke 11:53-54* RSV).

3) "When the people of Israel provoked the Lord in the wilderness for forty years, they perished" (*Hebrews 3:17*).

53. Kuleska masozi

To wipe away tears

Expl: The condolences given to the bereaved are symbolically considered as wiping away the tears of those who mourn.

Meaning: To comfort the bereaved.

Occasion: Usually cited at funerals, when the master of ceremonies receives the gifts of condolence. Sometimes the proverb refers to an orphaned child. People will look at the live child as a consolation. Preachers use it to refer to God as one who wipes away the tears of those who mourn.

Related Biblical Themes and Stories:

1) "The sovereign Lord will destroy death forever! He will wipe away the tears from everyone's eyes" *(Isaiah 25:8).*

2) "Happy are those who mourn; God will comfort them" *(Matthew 5:4).*

54. Kulinda malinda-linda

To wait for trouble

Expl: A person should try to take initiative instead of just sitting idle.

Meaning: One should not wait indefinitely for a good job or a better deal, lest such waiting lead one into unbearable suffering and misery.

Occasion: Cited when encouraging people to do whatever is available to earn their living, instead of waiting for good jobs or deals that may not be forthcoming. Sometimes it is used to warn those who always rely on others to do things for them, without themselves taking the lead. It is also used to advise farmers not to wait for too long before they plant their crops during the first rains. It can be used to exhort people to respond to the gospel immediately.

Related Biblical Themes and Stories:

1) "The right time has come, and the Kingdom is near, turn away from your sins and believe the Good News" *(Mark 1:15).*

2) "Go and sell all you have and give the money to the poor and you will have riches in heaven, then come and follow me" *(Mark 10:21).*

3) "The angel said, 'There will be no more delay!'" *(Revelation 10:5).*

55. Kumuzi waku ndi kumuzi waku

Your home is your home

Expl: The people should maintain good relations with their kinsmen (relatives). In the colonial period, many Tonga people used to go to work in South Africa for many years, even forgetting their own homes and families. Life was sweet in their early years there, but when they were faced with problems, they were forced to come back, sometimes empty-handed. Some even died there.

Meaning: A person should not despise his/her own relatives (or original home), because a time may come when circumstances will force her/him to go back to them.

Occasion: Used when we advise young people who despise their homes or relatives. When they come back, we may reproach them before we receive them back. It is also advice given at a funeral if the people had received their dead kinsman who never thought of home during his lifetime. Preachers can use it to exhort people to prepare to go to heaven, their real home.

Related Biblical Themes and Stories:

1) "I want to be buried where my fathers are; carry me out of Egypt and bury me where they are buried" (*Genesis 47:30*).

2) The story of the prodigal son is a good example. He despised living with his father and elder brother at home. When he went to a far country, trouble came. He squandered all his money, and in the end became helpless. Life was unbearable. He could not withstand the problems he faced in the foreign land. He almost died from hunger. He then thought of going back home to his father, where he was kindly received (*Luke 15:11-32*).

3) "There is no permanent city for us here on earth" (*Hebrews 13:14*).

56. Kupaska nkhusunga

To give is to store

Expl: This proverb reflects the Tonga belief in the importance of interdependence, as opposed to individualism, as a way of life.

Meaning: Giving is a way of saving, because the people you give things to or the people you help will come to your aid in time of need.

Occasion: The proverb addresses the theme of generosity. It is normally used when praising someone for having given something to someone in need or when approving his/her intention to do so. Young people are taught to share things with others.

Related Biblical Themes and Stories:

1) "Do not store up riches for yourselves here on earth, where moths and rust destroy, and robbers break in and steal. Instead, store up riches for yourselves in heaven where moths and rust cannot destroy and robbers

can not break in and steal. For your heart will always be where your riches are" (*Matthew 6:19-21*).

2) "If you only knew what God gives and who it is that is asking you for a drink, you would ask him, and he would give you life-giving water" (*John 4:10*).

3) "It is more blessed to give than to receive" (*Acts 20:35*).

4) "Each one should give, then as he has decided, not with regret or out of a sense of duty; for God loves the one who gives gladly. And God is able to give you more than you need" (*2 Corinthians 9:7-8*).

57. Kupereka mphepeska

To give a propitiatory offering

Expl: In Tonga traditional worship, some offerings were given as an appeasement to the spirits of the dead.

Meaning: Sometimes people make offerings to cause a spirit stop doing something hostile.

Occasion: Used when referring to a gift paid for appeasement. Preachers use it when referring to the offerings given to God as thanksgiving.

Related Biblical Themes and Stories:

1) The idea is that of sin offerings to God (*Leviticus 5:1-13*).

2) "A curse is on all of you because the whole nation is cheating me. Bring the full amount of your tithes to the Temple, so that there will be plenty of food there. I will open the windows of heaven and pour out on you in abundance all kinds of good things" *(Malachi 3:9-11)*.

58. Kurgha zina

To eat the name

Expl: It is the Tonga way of inheriting a name which is also a title to office.

Meaning: The successor to a name and a title of maternal uncle.

Occasion: Cited when choosing a person who should take the title of the clan name or become the next Chief.

Related Biblical Themes and Stories:

1) "And thou didst get thee a name as it is to this day" *(Nehemiah 9:10 RSV).*

2) "For he has fixed a day in which he will judge the whole world with justice by means of a man he has chosen" *(Acts 17:31).*

3) "To him who conquers I will give some of the hidden manna and I will give him a white stone, with a new name written on the stone which no one knows except him who receives it" *(Revelation 2:17, 3:5).*

59. Kuronde ndi manja ghawi

To receive with two hands

Expl: The Tonga people are generous, and this is shown in the way they treat their visitors and strangers. For instance, to care for someone is often expressed as keeping that person supplied with *dendi* (fish). Meat from game and chickens are a relish for visitors and special occasions.

Meaning: A person should be generous or hospitable to visitors.

Occasion: Cited when receiving important visitors, such as a Chief or political leaders or other important visitors. Preachers cite the proverb during the Christmas season. Jesus is an important visitor to our homes and should be received by everyone wholeheartedly, though we may not see him physically. Our celebrations should acknowledge his coming.

Related Biblical Themes and Stories:

1) "Some, however did receive him and believed in him; so he gave them the right to become God's children" *(John 1:12).*

2) "So if you consider me you partner, receive him as you would receive me" *(Philemon 17 RSV).*

3) "Keep on loving one another as Christian brothers. Remember to welcome strangers in your homes" *(Hebrews 13:1-2).*

60. Kuruta mphichi ndi kayuni

To go like a stick that misses a bird

Expl: The analogy depicts something that disappears and does not come back. If a person throws an object aiming to kill a bird and misses it, the object does not come back. The bird, too, flies away.

Meaning: A person should make an attempt to come back and thank those who helped him/her when he/she was in trouble.

Occasion: Cited to admonish those who take things for granted and do not appreciate what others have done for them. It can be used to teach Christians to give thanks for what others have done for them.

Related Biblical Themes and Stories:

1) Jesus said "There were ten men who were healed; where are the other nine? Why is this foreigner the only one who came back to give thanks to God?" *(Luke 17:17-18).*

2) "Everything you do or say, then, should be done in the name of the Lord Jesus, as you give thanks through him to God the Father" *(Colossians 3:17).*

61. Kusewe ndi chirwani mbuzereza

To play with danger is foolishness

Expl: This is from a legend that a person tamed a leopard. When it grew up, it killed all his goats, and even the master himself.

Meaning: A person should be careful what he/she does, eg. don't fool yourself HIV/AIDS kills.

Occasion: Cited to warn people against imitating silly habits which may end up ruining their lives. It is also a warning against apostasy. Elders cite it to warn young people not to play with danger or things that can ruin their lives. Preachers use it to warn people against the wrath of God.

Related Biblical Themes and Stories:

1) "They are saying that this is their god, who led them out of Egypt. I know how stubborn these people are. Now, don't try to stop me. I am angry with them, and I am going to destroy them" *(Exodus 32:7-10).*

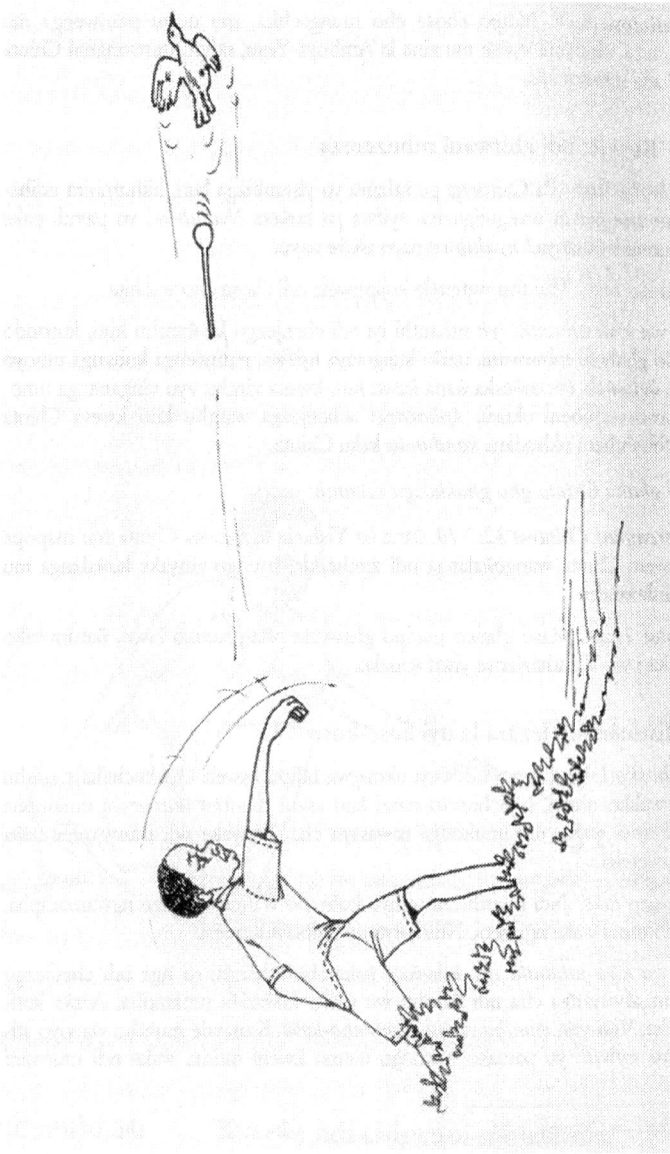

Proverb 60: Kuuta mphichi ndi kayuni
(To go like a stick that misses a bird)

Proverb 61: Kusewe ndi chirwani mbuzereza
(To play with danger is foolishness e.g. HIV/AIDS)

62. Kusewe ndi lezara la uyi kose-kose.

Playing with a double-edged blade.

Expl: The proverb is used symbolically. We should avoid taking for granted people we do not know well, since evil intention may lie in their hearts.

Meaning: A hypocrite or a liar.

Occasion: Used to advise a person to be careful in his/her dealings with someone known to be a liar. Sometimes the proverb is used to warn those people who blindly associate themselves with known witches or wizards in the community.

Related Biblical Themes and Stories:

1) "In that day the Lord will shave with a razor which is hired beyond the river—with the King of Assyria—the head and the hair of the feet, and it will sweep away the beard also" (*Isaiah 8:20*).

2) "Behold, you are relying on Egypt, that broken reed of staff, which will pierce the hand of man who leans on it" (*Isaiah 36:6* RSV).

63. Kutaya thayu

To pay vengeance or return evil for evil

Expl: There is a Tonga tale about a bush cat which killed itself just because it was tricked by a rooster. Later on, the kittens discovered that the cause of their father's death was the rooster. From that time, the bush cat has always sought to revenge their father's death. The English equivalent is "An eye for an eye."

Meaning: To return evil to someone.

Occasion: Often spoken when people intend to take vengeance on others.

Related Biblical Themes and Stories:

1) "You have heard that it was said, 'An eye for and eye, and tooth for tooth. But I say to you. Do not resist one who is evil. But if any one strikes you on the right cheek, turn to him the other also;" (*Matthew 5:38-39* RSV).

2) A clear example of revenge is that of Simon Peter who had a sword, drew it and struck the High Priest's slave, cutting off his right ear (*John 18:10*).

3) "Never take revenge, my friends, but instead let God's anger do it" *(Romans 12:19)*.

64. Kutorana ndi Viyuni Marambo

To be married by *Viyuni Marambo*

Expl: *Viyuni Marambo* is symbolically used to refer to migrated birds supposed to have originated from *Marambo*, which is a traditional name for Zambia, as the Tonga used to call it. It originates from a tale about a disobedient girl who got married to an unknown person. This man eventually grew wings and flew out over the sea with the girl. Then he disappeared into the sea, leaving her helpless in the middle of the sea.

Meaning: People should take heed of instructions and advice in order to avoid trouble in the end.

Occasion: Cited when warning young people against wasting their time on that which will not help them in the future. Often, girls who go early into marriage are ridiculed with this proverb for their inability to make a good choice.

Related Biblical Themes and Stories:

1) "Be not envious of evil men nor desire to be with them" *(Proverbs 24:1)*.

2) Paul mentions many evil ways that people fall into, and states that people who do such things will not get very far, because everyone will see they are stupid *(II Timothy 3:1-9)*.

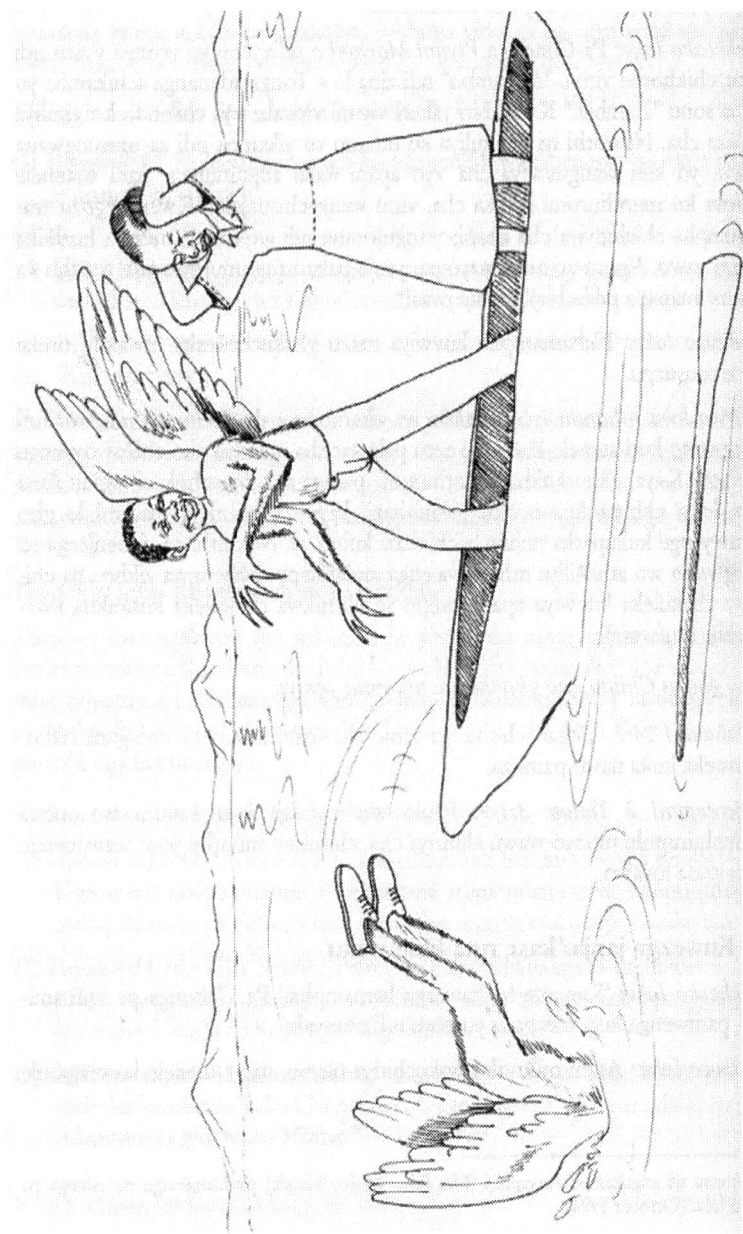

Proverb 64: Kutorana ndi Viyuni Marambo
(To be married by Viyuni Marambo)

65. Kuwezga janja or, Kase ruta kase weku

To return a hand

Expl: This is similar to the English saying, "One good turn deserves another." We should do what we expect others to do for us. In Tonga society, life is interdependent.

Meaning: Do something good to a person who did something good to you.

Occasion: Used to advise people not to keep on seeking favours, but to think of ways of assisting others also. Young people should learn the principle of reciprocity. Preachers can use the proverb when teaching on generosity and reciprocity.

Related Biblical Themes and Stories:
1) "Do for others what you want them to do for you" (*Matthew 7:12*).

66. Kuwika mphoro mlandu

To postpone a case

Expl: Mphoro is *sima* (thick porridge), which is kept overnight so that it can be served for children as their breakfast.

Meaning: To keep something for the future.
Occasion: Cited when hearing a case which might need postponement because of lack of evidence. Preachers can use it to stress the opposite, to show that some decisions should not be postponed, such as answering the call of Christ.

Related Biblical Themes and Stories:
1) Felix would postpone discussions with Paul, hoping that Paul would give him some money: "Go away for the present; when I have an opportunity I will summon you" (*Acts 24:25-26* RSV).

2) "When they had appointed a day for him, they cam to him at his lodging in great numbers. And he expounded the matter to them from morning to evening" (*Acts 2:23* RSV). In this sense the Council postponed to hear from Paul again.

3) "Listen! This is the hour to receive God's favour; today is the day to be saved!" (*II Corinthians 6:2*).

67. Kuyambiriya nkhugona pakati

Be early, you will sleep in the middle

Expl: The English equivalent is "An early bird catches the worm." Thus, if you want a big share, you should be early.

Meaning: Begin eradicating a problem before it gets worse. For instance, you should treat the wound before it gets infected.

Occasion: The proverb addresses the idea of preparedness. It is used to advise young people to plan for their future in the early stages in their lives. Also, in order to avoid contracting epidemic diseases, people are advised to take preventative measures. Likewise, school children are advised to be punctual so they do not miss their lessons. Our great duty is to watch, especially when things seem to be uncertain.

Related Biblical Themes and Stories:

1) The five foolish virgins were not fully prepared. When they arrived late, they found the door already closed, and the five clever virgins had already been welcomed by the bridegroom (*Matthew 25:1-13*).

2) The people who were late to come and listen to hear Jesus' message were kept out, for there were so many people who came together that there was no room left not even out in front of the door (*Mark 2:2*).

68. Kwambiriya maji gheche mugongono

You should cross a stream before the floods come

Expl: The analogy is drawn from a stream that rises gradually on a rainy day, and if one is late to cross, one can be carried away by the floods. The English equivalent is, "A stitch in time saves nine."

Meaning: Start solving a problem before it gets worse. That is, a problem should be attended to in its initial stages.

Occasion: The proverb has to do with decision-making. It is used to advise young people to effect some remedy before a thing gets worse. For instance, students should make their right choices from the early stages of education, such as in choosing subjects for their future career. Sometimes the proverb is cited to warn young people against acquiring habits that can undermine their future, e.g., smoking and drinking. If these habits are not controlled from the early stage, it will be very difficult to eradicate them when they are rooted in a person. It is also used in advising a person to promptly attend to a problem (e.g., that of disciplining his/her children) which the adviser fears may grow out of proportion and thus become impossible to manage, if left for long. Preachers can use it to stress the urgency of the gospel, just as Jesus warns us that there is no time to spare for burying the dead or for saying good-bye to a family.

Related Biblical Themes and Stories:

1) The prophet Isaiah says, "Seek the Lord while you can find him. Call upon him now while he is near" (*Isaiah 55:6*).

2) Jesus said, "Anyone who starts to plow and then keeps looking back is of no use for the Kingdom of God" (*Luke 9:57-62*).

69. Kwawiyako Chiuta

God has fallen on them there

Expl: In Tonga tradition, lightning or any other terrifying phenomenon in nature is associated with the nature of God. Disease is frequently so spoken of. God is seen as punishing people by inflicting diseases on them.

Meaning: The epidemic has wiped out the inhabitants of a place.

Occasion: Cited to acknowledge the presence of God. It is used to warn people against committing evil because God will visit them by sending plagues to wipe them out. Preachers use this proverb when they refer to the outbreak of diseases as God's will to punish sinners. Young people are warned against doing evil things, lest God send epidemics to wipe out people as a punishment.

Related Biblical Themes and Stories:

1) The proverb reflects the situation of Israel in Egypt when God inflicted the Egyptians with boils that became open sores on the people and the animals (*Exodus 9:8-10*).

2) "If I had raised my hand to strike you and your people with disease, you would have been completely destroyed" (*Exodus 9:15*).

3) "An angel of the Lord went to the Assyrian camp and killed 185,000 soldiers. At dawn the next day there they lay, all dead" (*Isaiah 37:36*).

4) "Does disaster strike a city unless the Lord sends it?" (*Amos 3:6*).

5) "There will be terrible earthquakes, famines, and plagues everywhere, there will be strange and terrifying things coming from the sky" (*Luke 21:11*).

70. Kwe karakato

There is one risen

Expl: There is a belief in Tonga society that some people rise from the dead in another form, e.g., a lion or a leopard.

Meaning: A person who overcomes death.

Occasion: Cited during situations when a strange wild animal such as a lion or leopard roars within the vicinity of a village. People feel this can be a person who is reincarnated in that particular animal. Preachers cite it to refer to the resurrection of Jesus.

Related Biblical Themes and Stories:

1) Jesus has authority over death. This is seen in the story of raising Lazarus from the dead. "Jesus called out in a loud voice, 'Lazarus come out.' He came out, his hands and feet wrapped in grave clothes, and with a cloth around his face. 'Untie him, and let him go'" (*John 11:43-44*).

2) Jesus' resurrection story can be illustrated by this proverb. Jesus is the one who conquers death (*John 20:1-10*).

71. Likhwechu lamunyako payika, mawa le pako

A whip used on someone else should be put away or tomorrow the same whip will be used to whip you

Expl: The same judgment you give to others will also be passed on you. The proverb is used symbolically.

Meaning: We should not rejoice at the bad fortune of others.

Occasion: The proverb addresses the theme of judgment. It is cited when judging cases at the court. The acquitted should not look with contempt on the one who has lost the case, because next time it could be himself/herself. Again, young people should not rejoice over the fate of others. There is no need to pay vengeance on other people.

Related Biblical Themes and Stories:

1) "Jesus said, 'Do not judge others, so that God will not judge you, for God will judge you in the same way you judge others, and he will apply to you the same rules you apply to others'" (*Matthew 7:1*).

2) "Never take revenge, my friends, but instead let God's anger do it. For the scripture says, Do not take revenge, my friends, but leave room for God's wrath, for it is written: "It is mine to avenge; I will repay," says the Lord (*Romans 12:19*).

72. Lilime lenge moto

The tongue is like fire

Expl: The tongue is here used metaphorically to indicate that little things can sometimes become uncontrollable.

Meaning: A person should be careful in handling small things.

Occasion: It is used to advise a person to be cautious of what he/she says in a group. Especially, that a person should control his/her temper, in order to reach a harmonious decision. Preachers have used this proverb to condemn divisions in their congregations.

Related Biblical Themes and Stories:

1) "Behold, the name of the Lord comes from far burning with his anger, and in thick rising smoke; his lips are full of indignation, and his tongue is like a devouring fire" (*Isaiah 30:27* RSV).

2) "Like fire they eat up the plants. In front of them the land is like the Garden of Eden, but behind them it is a barren desert" (*Joel 2:3*).

3) "Likewise the tongue is a small part of the body, but it makes great boasts" (*James 3:5*).

73. Limphezi liweliyamo cha mu chimiti

Lightning does not strike the same tree twice

Expl: There are things that happen once in a lifetime.

Meaning: Chance does not repeat itself.

Occasion: The proverb addresses the theme of responsibility. It is used to advise young people to take care of things they have or the chances they have. For instance, if one has acquired wealth, it is important not to be extravagant.

Related Biblical Themes and Stories:

1) "Do those things that will show that you have turned from your sins. The ax is ready to cut down the trees at the roots, every tree that does not bear good fruit will be cut down and thrown in the fire" (*Matthew 3:8-12*).

2) The parable of the prodigal son can be illustrated by this proverb. When the son spent all the wealth he received from his father, he ended up being helpless. He lost all his chances and ended up starving (*Luke 15:11-21*).

3) "Therefore, we should hold fast with what we have lest one takes it away" (*Revelation 3:11*).

74. Maliro nkhuliyana

A funeral is to mourn one another

Expl: In Tonga society no person is an island. The people are interdependent.

Meaning: People should help each other in times of trouble.

Occasion: Cited to urge people who stay aloof to offer charitable services to those who mourn or fall into trouble, e.g., in burying the dead or helping others in times of disaster. This participation is important because next time one would need similar help when facing the same problem. Young people should learn to offer some help at a funeral; e.g., digging the grave or running errands.

Related Biblical Themes and Stories:

1) In the Sermon on the Mount, Jesus said, "Whatever you wish that men would do to you, do so to them" (*Matthew 7:12b*).

2) Another related story from the Bible is that of Jesus raising Lazarus from the dead (*John 11:1-44*). Verses 31-34 present a similar picture of the neighbouring Jews coming to console and weep with Mary and Martha for the death of Lazarus.

3) Finally, Paul in his letter to the Thessalonians advises them to comfort one another (*I Thessalonians 4:18*).

75. Malo gho utanja kusambapo ndigho patachikukole mng'ona

The bathing place you like best brings a crocodile bite

Expl: We should be careful with our lives lest we are overtaken by events.

Meaning: Danger may exist where you least expect it.

Occasion: Used to warn people against carelessness or against taking things for granted. Thus, young people should be responsible and be sensitive to situations. They should avoid going to places that attract them but which are full of danger, e.g., drinking places.

Related Biblical Themes and Stories:

1) "An evil spirit from God suddenly took control of Saul and he raved in his house like a madman. David was playing the harp as he did everyday and Saul was holding a spear. 'I'll pin him to the wall,' Saul said to himself, and he threw the spear at him twice; but David dodged each time" (*I Samuel 18:10-11*).

76. Manda ghawole pa khomo

In tranquility lies danger

Expl: "*Manda*" is a type of mushroom usually growing around homes. In most cases people do not know that there is mushroom in the vicinity until it gets rotten. Then they discover it.

Meaning: A person should not take for granted that things are always as they are. Danger is inevitable in any place.

Occasion: Used to discourage people from taking chances without thinking. For instance, one should not take chances by walking alone at night just because there is light in the area, nor leave the door of the house open because there are no wild animals or thieves about. Young people are warned against travelling alone in the dark or against frequenting places they feel there can be danger.

Related Biblical Themes and Stories:

The proverb addresses being responsible.

1) "Be on watch, be alert, for you do not know when the time will come" (*Mark 13:32-36*).

2) In the parable of the rich fool, we are warned that when things go well with us we should also know that death is near us. "You fool, this very night you will have to give up your life" (*Luke 12:20*).

77. Mata gha Mula ghatuwa pasi cha

An old person's saliva cannot fall to the ground

Expl: What an old person has said will one day come true. The old person's saying in Tonga society is supposed to be taken seriously. There is a tale about young people who killed all the old people. One young man hid his old father in a cave. One day trouble came upon their young Chief. As he woke up from sleep, he saw a snake that rolled round his neck. The young people needed a solution to save their Chief. It was the old man who gave wise advice and the Chief's life was spared.

Meaning: The old are the wise.

Occasion: The proverb relates to the theme of obedience. It is told to induce the young to respect the views of their elders or to reprimand those who find themselves in great trouble after ignoring their elders' advice. Preachers can use the proverb to stress the need to obey God. God is depicted as ancient and wise. His words do not fail. What is spoken from the mouth of the Lord shall come to pass.

Related Biblical Themes and Stories:

1) Eli's warning to his two sons came true. Hophni and Phinehas were both killed just as Eli had told his sons (*I Samuel 4:11* and *2:25*).

2) God's word through angel Gabriel to Mary can be referred to here: "For there is nothing that God cannot do" (*Luke 1:37*).

78. Matako ghawi ghaleka cha ku kwenthana

Two buttocks cannot avoid friction

Expl: People should learn to live together in spite of any problems they might have.

Meaning: Misunderstandings are unavoidable where there are two or more people living together.

Occasion: The setting of the proverb is in a court when elders try to reconcile people who have either quarreled or fought each other, e.g., husband and wife or two villages in friction. Children in a family are advised to live together despite the disagreements which may occur.

Related Biblical Themes and Stories:

1) The proverb can be related to the story about Abraham (Abram) and Lot quarreling over land. "Lot also had sheep, goats, and cattle, as well as his own family and servants. And so there was not enough pasture land for the two of them to stay together, because they had too many animals. So quarrels broke out between the men who took care of Abram's animals and those who took care of Lot's animals" (*Genesis 13:5-7*).

2) "An argument broke out among the disciples as to which one of them should be thought of as the greatest" (*Luke 22:24*).

3) There arose a sharp argument that led to the separation between Paul and Barnabas. It is reported that Barnabas wanted to take John Mark with them, but Paul did not think it was right to take him because he had not stayed with them to the end of their mission in Pamphylia. There was a sharp argument between them, and they separated. Barnabas took Mark and Paul chose Silas and left (*Acts 15:39-40*).

79. Maungu tikumwa, matali tikurhga! Kwajanji so?

We have supped of the marrows and eaten the mushroom! What is remaining now?

Expl: It is a form of thanksgiving prayer to God for fruits and fungi growing wild in the woods, of which Tonga are very fond and eat as plants of God.

Meaning: A person should consider himself/herself safe having eaten the gifts of heaven with thankfulness.

Occasion: Used during Tonga traditional worship as a thanksgiving prayer to God as the Giver of the Rain. To Him alone this *Chiwi* or "rain-prayer" should be offered with hope for the new life. Preachers use this in their prayers of thanksgiving for the first rains.

Related Biblical Themes and Stories:

1) This proverb can be related to the creed recited on harvest offerings: "My ancestor was a wandering Aramean who took his family to Egypt to live ... The Egyptians treated us harshly and forced us to work as slaves ... He brought us out of Egypt and gave us this rich and fertile

land. And behold now I bring the first of the fruit of the ground which the Lord has given me" (*Deuteronomy 26:5-10*).

2) "Behold I have given you every plant yielding seed which is upon the face of all the earth and every tree with seed in its fruits; you shall have them for food" (*Genesis 1:29*).

80. Mawala ghatuswa vyaka

Pride leads one to break hoe-handles

Expl: There are people who pretend to be wise or able to do things, yet they turn out to be foolish in the end and can spoil things.

Occasion: The proverb addresses the theme of modesty. It is cited to warn young people who have big intentions before they can actually acquire the skills of doing things properly. If the advice is not heeded, they end up destroying things or other people's lives.

Related Biblical Themes and Stories:

1) "People who are proud will soon be disgraced. It is wiser to be modest" (*Proverbs 11:2*).

2) "Pride goes before destruction, and a haughty spirit before a fall." (*Proverbs 16:18*).

3) "Your pride has deceived you" (*Jeremiah 49:16*).

81. Mawonekedu ghanyenga

Appearance is deceptive

Expl: We should not go for beauty but quality. A person can be beautiful but lazy.

Meaning: Beauty is nothing compared to quality of work.

Occasion: Cited when advising a young person to be careful in choosing a future partner. Preachers use it to advise Christians not to be drawn away by things which appear attractive but which can be sources of danger.

Related Biblical Themes and Stories:

1) "Go in through the narrow gate, because the gate to hell is wide and the road that leads to it is easy, and there are many who travel it. But the

gate to life is narrow and the way that leads to it is hard, and there are few people who find it" *(Matthew 7:13-14)*.

2) "For the love of money is a source of all kinds of evil. Some have been so eager to have it that they have wandered away from the faith and have broken their hearts with many sorrows" *(I Timothy 6:10)*.

82. Mazu gha wala ghawe pawaka cha

Words of old people become fulfilled after a long time

Expl: The Tonga believe there are sages in their community whose wisdom and advice should be adhered to. These wise people are the source of moral and spiritual wisdom.

Meaning: What the old people say always comes true in the end, although the young may despise the saying or the warning.

Occasion: Normally used by old people who are resigned to a young person's decision. The older people will emphasize their advice or warnings to the younger all the same. When judging cases, the jury may utter such a proverb, to fulfill some advice or warning that was given to the accused earlier.

Related Biblical Themes and Stories:

1) The story of Eli and his two sons can be illustrated by this proverb. The warnings of Eli to his sons Hophni and Phinehas came to be true in the end (*Samuel 2:22-25 and Samuel 4:10-11*).

2) On many occasions, prophets warned the people of Israel about impending dangers, yet the people did not believe that the prophecies would come true. For instance, in Isaiah 8:16-18, Isaiah had to give up when people refused to listen to his advice. But in the end, Judah was devastated by the Assyrians. Isaiah's words were fulfilled *(Isaiah 36:1-2)*.

3) Jesus also warned his disciples about the fate Jerusalem would suffer (*Mark 13:1-23*). This was fulfilled when Pompey destroyed Jerusalem in 70 AD. The word of God shall always come to pass.

83. Mazu gha wala ghayanana ndi sabora wakali mweniyo wawawa cha

The words from elders are like old chili (spice), which does not turn sour

Expl: People should heed the advice of the elders.

Meaning: A wise saying reconciles a disturbed mind; therefore, one should not show contempt for old people's wisdom.

Occasion: Cited when advising young people to follow the advice of older people.

Related Biblical Themes and Stories:

1) "My son, keep my words and treasure up my commandments with you; keep my commandments and live" *(Proverbs 7:1)*.

2) "My son, be attentive to my wisdom, incline your ear to my understanding that you may keep discretion" *(Proverbs 5:1-2)*.

84. Mazua ghasintha

Days always change

Expl: People should learn to be interdependent as opposed to living independent lives.

Meaning: Life cannot be consistent. There are ups and downs in life.

Occasion: Used to urge people who are privileged to help the underprivileged ones, since they may one day require the services of these same people when fortunes change. Politicians usually use it in their campaigning for change and warn the electorate about future consequences when the pendulum swings to the opposition side. Young people should be sensitive to the changes of the time they live in. Preachers may use the proverb to give hope of better days in the future through God's grace.

Related Biblical Themes and Stories:

1) "Never boast about tomorrow, you don't know what will happen between now and then" *(Proverbs 27:1)*.

2) Jerusalem will be restored in the latter days *(Isaiah 4:2-6)*.

3) Many prophets who rose in Israel believed that days would not always be the same. Amos proclaimed that the "Day of the Lord" would come and it would be a fearful one *(Amos 5:16-20)*. And then "A day is coming when I will restore the Kingdom of David which is a house fallen into ruins" *(Amos 9:11)*. Isaiah also talks about times of chaos in Jerusalem *(Isaiah 3:1-6)*.

85. Mazua nganande, weya wang'ombe njumana

Days are more than a cow's hair

Expl: Desist from disappointing others through showing them harshness on matters that can be solved, because you will still meet somewhere one day, and you will be ashamed of yourself.

Meaning: It is not good to disappoint another person, since you are also bound to get into trouble one day and may fail to get sympathy or assistance.

Occasion: The proverb has to do with reconciliation and forgiveness. It is used to advise young people to reconcile with others when things have gone wrong between them. Sometimes it is used by a person who has been disappointed by a colleague, as an indication of one's resolve to pay something owed. It can be used in sermons on forgiveness or reconciliation.

Related Biblical Themes and Stories:

1) Jesus said, "If you are about to offer your gift to God at the altar and there you remember that your brother has something against you, leave your gift there in front of the altar go at once and make peace with your brother and then come back and offer your gift to God" (*Matthew 5:23-24*).

2) "My brothers, if someone is caught in any kind of wrong doing, those of you who are spiritual should set him right; but you must do it in a gentle way. And keep an eye on yourselves, so that you will not be tempted, too" (*Galatians 6:1*).

86. Mbawa kume masengwe nkhuwambala lisito

A cautious deer grows longer horns

Expl: If a deer wants to live long enough to grow impressive horns, it must be very careful with its life. The Tonga traditional way to kill game was to dig game-pits and cover them with branches. If an animal does not avoid the hedge, then it will fall into the pit. The safest way is to avoid it.

Meaning: If one wants to live long, one must be careful. People who are cautious avoid unnecessary danger.

Occasion: Usually used in contemporary situations in which students sometimes blindly or ignorantly find themselves participating in ill-conceived boycotts or violence. In the end, they are expelled from school. It is also cited to warn young people to be careful in the way they move with their peers, so that they may not ruin their lives.

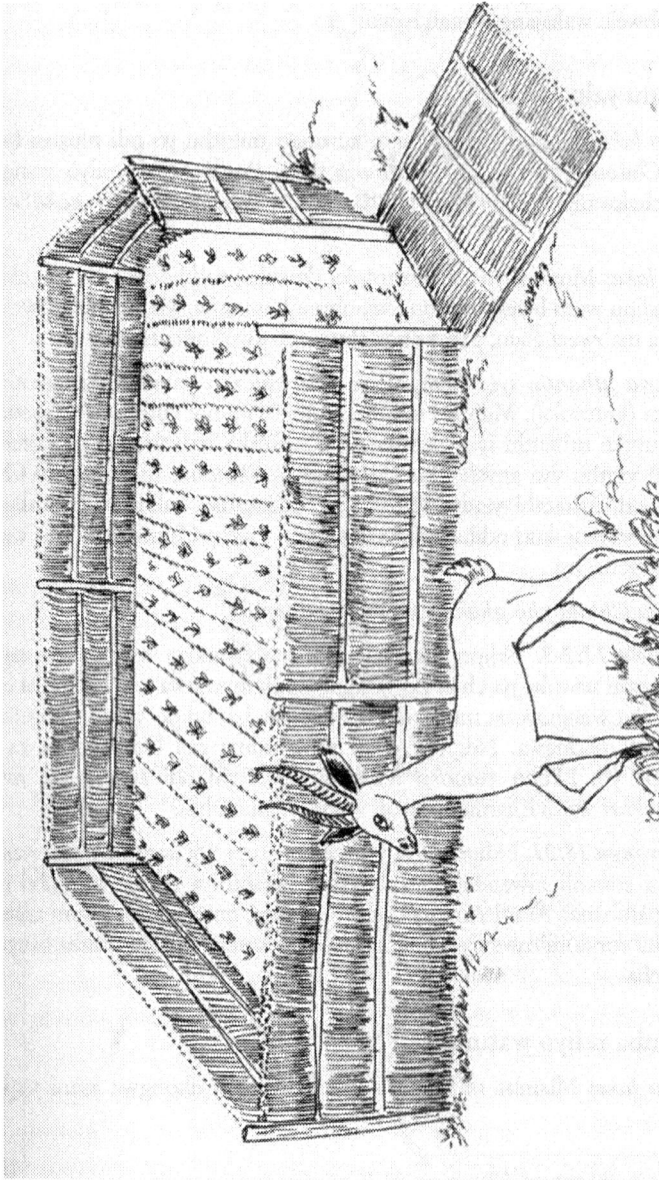

Proverb 86: Mbawa kume masengwe mkhuwambala lisitu
(A cautious deer grows longer horns)

Related Biblical Themes and Stories:
1) "Wisdom will add years to your life" (*Proverbs 9:11*).
2) "Have reverence for the Lord and you will live longer. The wicked die before their time" (*Proverbs 10:27*).
3) "If you love your life, stay away from the traps that catch the wicked along the way" (*Proverbs 22:5*).

87. Mbunu yaku Pundu

A hyena's greed

Expl: It is used metaphorically to refer to a person who is selfish. There is a folktale which says that a hyena burst its stomach because it could not choose between two paths for his hunt.

Meaning: A person who is greedy is not satisfied with one thing.

Occasion: Used to warn against selfishness. A person should be contented with what he/she has. Preachers often use it to warn Christians against being double-dealers. They should choose to live a good life.

Related Biblical Themes and Stories:
1) The story about Ahab and Elijah on Mount Carmel: "And Elijah came near to all the people, and said, 'How long will you go limping with two different opinions? If the Lord is God, follow him; but if Baal, then follow him'" (*I Kings 18:21*).

2) "I know that you are neither cold nor hot. How I wish you were either one or the other! But because you are luke warm, neither hot nor cold, I am going to spit you out of my mouth!" *(Revelation 3:15-16)*.

88. Mkucha nkhazunguliyanga chulu

Another day I will be wandering round a heap

Expl: The Tonga belief that the corpse turns into a heap (*chulu*), i.e., the old grave becomes a heap.

Meaning: A person who is beyond and outside, as in death.

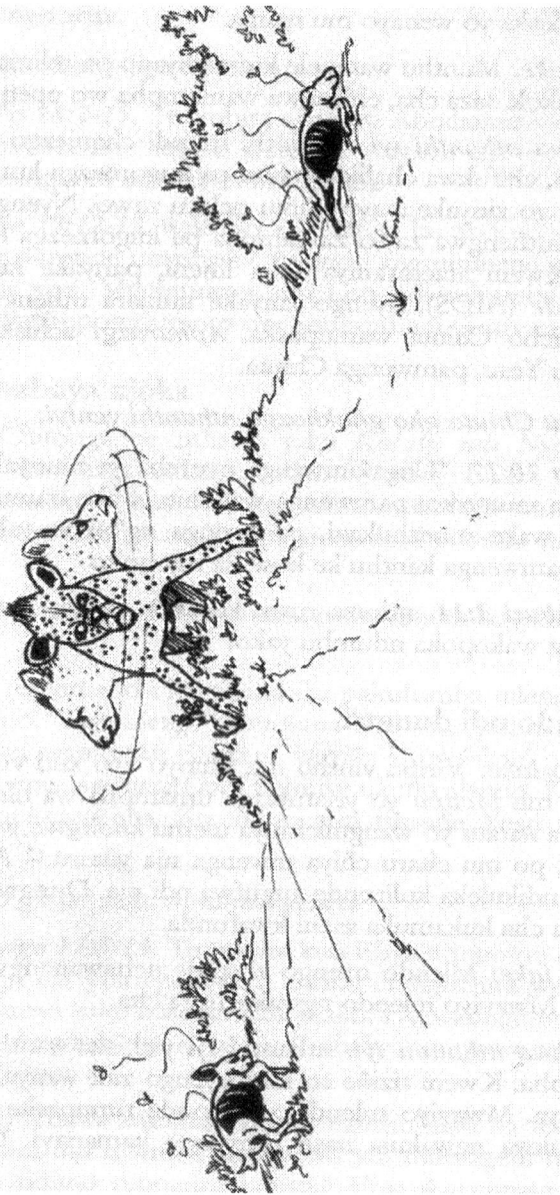

Proverb 87: Mbumu yaku pundu
(Hyena's greed)

Occasion: Used to warn a child as to his/her behaviour and to make the advice more impressive.

Related Biblical Themes and Stories:

1) When Jesus predicted his death, he said, "A little while and you will see me no more, again a little while and you will see me" (*John 16:16*).

2) In speaking about his death, Jesus also said, "Do not forget what I am about to tell you! The Son of Man is going to be handed over to the power of men" (*Luke 9:44*).

89. Mlamba ndiyo watunga

The mudfish is what you have in your hand.

Expl: The mudfish is usually very slippery while in water. Hence once it is caught, one must hold it tight; one should not be deceived by the fish wriggling in water. What is yours is what you have in your hands. The English equivalent is "A bird in the hand is worth two in the bush."

Meaning: A person should concentrate on what he/she is supposed to do. You should not dispense with an old thing or relationship or abandon your job just because you hope to acquire a seemingly more attractive one.

Occasion: Used to caution young people who act in an envious manner at the time their hopes fail to materialise or when their newly acquired things or relationships prove worthless. In early marital life, young people tend to despise their wives when they look at other young girls and feel like divorcing their old wives. It is also a warning to young people who are greedy. In other words, one should be satisfied with what one has. Students are advised not to turn away from their main function of learning.

Related Biblical Themes and Stories:

1) This proverb can apply to the tenth commandment: "Do not desire another man's house; do not desire his wife, his slave, his cattle, his donkey or anything else that he owns" (*Exodus 20:17*).

2) In Revelation 3:11, we are advised to "Keep safe what you have, so that no one will rob you of your victory prize."

90. Mlendo ndi dungwi

A visitor is like dew

Expl: Certain things in life are short-lived. There is a Tonga folktale about an old man and three boys. The one who welcomed the visitor received blessings. Those who rejected him died of hunger.

Meaning: A stranger is a blessing, and stays for a short time. So we should not regard visitors as a bother.

Occasion: Cited when advising young people who are hostile to strangers, to welcome them to their homes. A stranger is not a bother.

Related Biblical Themes and Stories:

1) When Abraham saw the three visitors coming to him, he ran out to meet them. Bowing down with his face touching the ground he said, "Sirs, please do not pass by my home without stopping, I am here to serve you" (*Genesis 18:2-15*). The three strangers later on brought good news to Abraham and Sarah about the promised son. The visitors were not a bother to Abraham, but rather a blessing.

2) The visitors to Sodom and Gomorrah were welcomed by Lot: "The two men said to Lot, 'If you have anyone else here—sons, daughters, son-in-law, or any other relatives living in the city—get them out of here because we are going to destroy this place'" (*Genesis 19:12-13*).

3) "Remember to welcome strangers in your homes. There were some who did that and welcomed angels without knowing it" (*Hebrews 12:3*).

91. Mlendo ndiyo wabaya njoka

A visitor kills a snake

Expl: A visitor can be a help. This proverb is similar to a Tonga story referring to the hare and the leopard. While the council of elders (court) was in a deadlock over a case, the hare came from the bush and helped to pass judgment. The visitor can be more diplomatic.

Meaning: A visitor or traveller may have better discernment when there is a critical issue.

Occasion: Used when asking a visitor to help solve a problem when the local men seem to be entangled in a riddle. Young people should develop the spirit of being kind to strangers.

Related Biblical Themes and Stories:

In the story of Elijah and the Shunamite woman at Zarephath:

1) The prophet Elijah, a visitor at the time of great famine, helped the woman to have enough food after he had performed a miracle. At first the woman thought that by offering to the stranger her last meal, things would be worse for her and her son; but we see that the visitor became a blessing, giving a solution to her problem—always food was found in her jar (*I Kings 17:8-15*).

2) Elijah also restored the widow's son to life (*I Kings 17:23*).

3) Rahab and her family were protected because she received the two visitors (spies) in Jericho. Joshua then told the two men who served as spies, "Go into the prostitute's house and bring her and her family out, as you promised her" (*Joshua 6:22-23*).

92. Mnthenkhu waryiya pa chipando

The blackbird, mnthenkhu, eats while seated on a stump

Expl: Mnthenkhu is a small blackbird. The Tonga people have observed that each time this bird catches an insect, it looks for a stump or a branch to sit on and eat its prey. The proverb is used symbolically to imply self-respect.

Meaning: A person should respect himself/herself.

Occasion: Cited when advising young people to cultivate good manners or etiquette in a society. For instance, children like to eat while walking or standing, which is contrary to the norms of Tonga society.

Related Biblical Themes and Stories:

1) "Jesus said to him, 'Foxes have holes, and birds have nests, but the Son of Man has no place to lie down and rest'" (*Luke 9:58*).

2) Paul advised the Corinthians to respect themselves when he said, "If any one is hungry he should eat at home, so that you will not come under God's judgment as you meet together" (*I Corinthians 11:34*).

3) God rewards those people who do not show off (*Matthew 6:18*).

108

Proverb 92: Mnthenkhu waryiya pa chipando
(The blackbird, mnthenkhu, eats while seated on a stump)

93. Moto walimbuni utocha lisuwa likuru

A small fire destroys a big forest

Expl: We should be careful with little things because they can become dangerous and magnified.

Meaning: Small things can cause great damage.

Occasion: Used to advise people to take care of small inconveniences or embarrassments caused to others, since such provocations can cause bigger trouble or disaster. Usually young married couples are advised to take care of little issues that could lead to the breaking up of families. A person who inconveniences or embarrasses another over a minor issue is bound to find himself/herself in much bigger trouble.

Related Biblical Themes and Stories:

1) The proverb can be related to several analogies listed in the book of James *(James 3:3-10)*. We put a bit into the mouth of a horse to make it obey us and we are able to make it go where we want.

2) A ship, big as it is and driven by such strong winds, can be steered by a very small rudder, and it goes wherever the pilot wants it to go.

3) The tongue is like fire. It is a world of wrong occupying its place in our bodies and spreading evil through our whole being.

Proverb 93: Moto walimbuni utocha lisuwa likuru
(A small fire destroys a big forest)

94. Mtiti ungamugolore cha pa mazila ghake

A sparrow is never small around its eggs

Expl: A sparrow is the smallest bird in the world but when it wants to protect its eggs, it becomes so angry that other big birds cannot fly near it.

Meaning: Every person should be respected without regard to their size, position, race or sex.

Occasion: Used when cautioning a person who despises those who are under him/her just because he/she is in a higher position. The proverb is also used to warn people against taking other people's property just because they cannot defend themselves, forgetting that the owner can sue them in court.

Related Biblical Themes and Stories:

1) "Hammer the points of your plows into swords and your pruning knives into spears. Even the weak must fight" (*Joel 3:10*).

2) "God chose what the world considers weak in order to shame the powerful" (*I Corinthians 1:27*).

3) King David was condemned because he planned Uriah's death in order to take his wife (*2 Samuel 12:1-15*).

95. Mtonga nchigumbuli

A Tonga person is crafty

Expl: The proverb is used metaphorically. The metaphor is drawn from a very cunning small fish called *Chigumbuli* (a small spotted fish). It can easily adapt itself to certain situations. When danger comes, it can disguise itself or hide under the sand.

Meaning: A person should not be deliberately exposed to danger.

Occasion: Used to encourage young people to be intelligent, but also adapt to certain situations in life, e.g., to exist peacefully in undisciplined situations.

Related Biblical Themes and Stories:

1) "They had to be youths without blemish, handsome and skillful in all wisdom, endowed with knowledge, understanding and learning" (*Daniel 1:4*).

2) "So that we may no longer be children, tossed to and fro and carried about with every wind of doctrine, by the cunning of men" (*Ephesians 4:14*).

3) "Listen! I am sending you out just like sheep in the midst of wolves; so be wise as snakes and innocent as doves" (*Matthew 10:16*).

96. Mu moyo ndi mu sitolo

The womb is a store

Expl: The metaphor is used to show that children born from one mother cannot be the same. Their attitudes, behaviour and even appearance will be different.

Meaning: In every family there is a bad person, so no family should be condemned wholesale because of the existence of one bad individual within it.

Occasion: Used to advise those who condemn whole families or communities for breeding different members of the society, forgetting that people differ in many ways. It is important to accept such differences.

Related Biblical Themes and Stories:

1) The four sons of Jesse—Eliab, Abinadab, Shammah and David—were totally different people in the eyes of God, because God pays no attention to how tall and handsome a man is. God looks at the heart of a person (*I Samuel 16:6-13*).

2) It was one of the twelve disciples, Judas, who betrayed Jesus, though he was in Jesus' inner circle. (*Mark 14:45-46*).

3) The two sons of Isaac, Esau and Jacob, were totally different. Esau was a very skilled hunter, a man who loved outdoors, but Jacob was a quiet man who stayed at home (*Genesis 25:27*).

97. Munthu wambura kuvwa wabuchira mbavi ye mu mutu waki

A person who does not hear learns when the ax is in his head

Expl: A person should obey instructions without being forced to do so.

Meaning: A person should take heed of instructions and advice in order to avoid trouble.

Occasion: Used when warning disobedient and disrespectful children to abandon their bad habits.

Related Biblical Themes and Stories: The proverb is related to the theme of obedience.

1) "The disobedient will miss entering the Kingdom of God because they will be thrown out into the darkness, where they will cry and gnash their teeth" (*Matthew 8:12*).

2) "The message given to our ancestors by the angels was shown to be true, and anyone who did not follow it or obey it received the punishment he deserved" (*Hebrews 2:2*).

98. Munthu wamtimba kuwi

A person with a double heart

Expl: A person who goes to one person and says something, then comes to another and says something different.

Meaning: A liar or double-dealer.

Occasion: Cited to warn against associating with someone known to be a liar. It teaches young people the need for caution, and to avoid trusting too quickly people we do not know well, since behind their broad and seemingly friendly smiles may lie evil intentions.

Related Biblical Themes and Stories:

1) "All of them lie to one another, they deceive each other with flattery" (*Psalm 12:2*).

2) "Then Judas Iscariot, one of the twelve disciples went off to the chief priests in order to betray Jesus to them" (*Mark 14:10*).

3) "Deacons likewise must be serious, not double-tongued" (*I Timothy 3:8* RSV).

4) "A person like that, unable to make up his mind and undecided in all he does, must not think that he will receive anything from the Lord" (*James 1:8*).

99. Munthukazi wakuja pa khonde watuba vyaweni, po anyaki alima yiyu cha

A lazy woman ends up stealing food

Expl: There is no way you can eat something good unless you work for it. Survival means working hard.

Meaning: People work hard in order to lead good lives.

Occasion: Cited to advise young married couples to be responsible and strive to work hard for their lives. Lazy people are encouraged to be hardworking.

Related Biblical Themes and Stories:

1) "Hard work will give you power, being lazy will make you a slave" (*Proverbs 12:24*).

2) "If you are lazy, you will never get what you are after, but if you work hard, you will get a fortune" (*Proverbs 12:27*).

3) "If you are lazy, you will meet difficulty everywhere, but if you are honest, you will have no trouble" (*Proverbs 15:19*).

4) "A lazy person is as bad as someone who is destructive" (*Proverbs 18:9*).

5) "Go ahead and be lazy. Sleep on, but you will go hungry" (*Proverbs 19:15*).

6) "The lazy man stays at home; he says a lion might get him if he goes outside" (*Proverbs 22:13*).

100. Mutu dulika-dulika

To appear without carrying something on the head

Expl: The thought depicts a person who has a problem and wants some help.

Meaning: A person who needs support of some kind, but does not make proper use of it when it is given.

Occasion: Used to ridicule someone who at one time asked for some support and did not make proper use of it.

Related Biblical Themes and Stories:

1) The proverb is in line with the servant who received one talent and hid it without investing it in something. He came back empty-handed. "I went and hid your talent in the ground" *(Matthew 25:24-30)*.

2) The story of the prodigal son *(Luke 15:11-32)*.

101. Muyane ndi Chiuta

Be of one mind with God

Expl: The saying points to the Tonga traditional belief that there is inter-communication between the living and the spirits of the dead, who pass on the petitions of the living to the Supreme Spirit.

Meaning: A person should be like God.

Occasion: Cited by preachers when they want to exhort people to follow the examples of Jesus or to live exemplary lives that will be acceptable to God.

Related Biblical Themes and Stories:

1) "Love the Lord your God with all your heart, with all your soul, with all your mind, and with all your strength" *(Mark 12:30)*.

2) "Since you are God's dear children, you must try to be like him" *(Ephesians 5:1)*.

3) "Have this mind among yourselves which is yours in Christ Jesus" *(Philippians 2:5-6 RSV)*.

102. Mwana kopa kazimu nkhumuluma

A child fears an insect if it bites him/her

Expl: Children cannot judge what is good and bad until they gradually discover through experience.

Meaning: Experience is a good teacher. In other words, through accumulation of knowledge we have a better insight into things.

Occasion: Used to encourage young people to endure certain difficult circumstances because they will confront them throughout their lives. The proverb is also cited to warn people to be careful in the way they handle their lives. They are advised to keep away from things that can ruin them. People are warned not to do the same bad things over and over again.

Related Biblical Themes and Stories:

1) By experience Laban knew that God had blessed him through Jacob (*Genesis 30:27*).

2) Experience makes one far wiser than anyone (*Ecclesiastes 1:16*).

3) Throughout the story of Israel, God reminds them to remember their past experiences. "Remember this and consider, recall it to mind, you transgressors, remember the former things of old" (*Isaiah 46:8*).

4) The Lord Jesus warned us to learn from the experience of others and not remain in sin, otherwise we shall experience the same fate: "No indeed! And I tell you that if you do not turn from your sins, you all die as they did" (*Luke 13:5*).

5) "Now turn from your sins! If you don't, I will come to you soon and fight against those people with the sword that comes out of my mouth" (*Revelation 2:16*).

103. Mwana mranda wasambira vyo wanthu wakamba pa Mphara

An orphan child learns from what people say at the *Mphara*

Expl: *Mphara* is an open place (or venue for ad hoc meetings for men and young people) where jokes are shared. In Tonga society there is a story about two millipedes. One was orphaned. When the young millipede with a mother was being admonished, the orphan listened too, and learned. He did not have problems in his life in the end.

Meaning: If you want to be wise, listen to what wise people say as they gather around, and try to make use of such wisdom. In other words, a child should heed the advice directed to others.

Occasion: Cited when a person draws the attention of his disobedient child to some good advice given to another child by its parents or guardians. The intention is to teach children to take note of any good advice from whomever it may come.

Related Biblical Themes and Stories:

1) If young men listen to the advice, they will grow wise. If they follow good instructions from elderly people they will live a long and happy life. If they cling to wisdom, it will protect them (*Proverbs 14:1-6*).

2) "Teach a child how he should live and he will remember it all his life" (*Proverbs 22:6*).

104. Mwana ndi chola

A child is a bag

Expl: You cannot leave your own child behind when he/she is supposed to help you.

Meaning: A parent does not reject his child, even if the child offends him.

Occasion: Used to warn a person against being excessively rough with an offending child. Fathers usually take their children along during short errands because children might be useful in carrying things or to be sent elsewhere to take important messages.

Related Biblical Themes and Stories:

1) Abraham was asked to take his son Isaac to offer sacrifice at Moriah. Abraham made Isaac carry the wood for sacrifice (*Genesis 22:2-7*).

2) Children are a gift from the Lord, a real blessing. "The sons a man has when he is young are like arrows in a soldiers hand" (*Psalm 127:3*).

3) Parents, do not treat you children in such a way as to make them angry. Instead raise them with Christian discipline and instruction" (*Ephesians 6:4*).

105. Mwana wa m'malundi

A child of the legs

Expl: The proverb is used to indicate indirectly that someone is a slave. The origin of the Tonga saying is that a supplicating slave used to express his submission by holding his master's legs.

Meaning: He/she is a slave or a servant or a foreigner.

Occasion: Used as a gesture for passing on vital information in a way which is least likely to attract the attention of the person concerned.

Related Biblical Themes and Stories:

1) "A servant does not know what his master is doing" (*John 15:15*).

2) "A slave does not belong to a family permanently but a son belongs there forever" (*John 8:35*).

3) "Now Moses was faithful in all God's house as a servant, to testify to the things that were to be spoken later, but Christ was faithful over God's house as a son." *(Hebrews 3:5).*

4) "Like a slave longing for cool shade" *(Job 7:2).*

106. Mwana wachiti nyama walinga wayiwona

When a child says, "meat," he/she has seen it elsewhere

Expl: This is equivalent to the English proverb, "There is no smoke without fire." That is, there is always a cause of something.

Meaning: There is some truth in anything that many people constantly talk about.

Occasion: Used in a court setting, especially when many witnesses confirm before the jury the manner in which an incident occurred. In certain families the tendency is to keep things away from children. This is to prevent them from revealing to people what they have seen. When a child lets out a secret, people cite the proverb.

Related Biblical Themes and Stories:

1) "Whatever is covered up will be uncovered, and every secret will be made known. So then, whatever you have said in the dark will be heard in broad daylight, and whatever you have whispered in private in a closed room will be shouted from the housetops" *(Luke 12:2-3).*

2) "One of the High Priest's slaves, a relative of the man whose ear Peter had cut off, spoke up, 'Didn't I see you with him in the garden?' he asked. Again Peter said, 'No', and at once a rooster crowed" (John 18:26).

107. Mwana wakuti kaya kuti wachila cha

If you doubt about a child's health, then know the child will die

Expl: A thing that is doubted by many may still have some truth about it because of the many people who testify to it.

Meaning: There is some truth in anything that many people constantly talk about.

Occasion: Used in cases of chronic illnesses when people lose hope. The people are encouraged not to lose hope. Young people are advised to have courage when life seems to be hopeless and frustrating.

Related Biblical Themes and Stories:

1) "Jesus said to Thomas, 'Put your finger here and look at my hands, then reach out your hand and put it in my side. Stop your doubting and believe'" (*John 20:27*).

2) "But if he has doubts about what he eats, God condemns him when he eats it, because his action is not based on faith. And anything that is not based on faith is sin" (*Romans 14:23*).

108. Mwana wambula kuvwa wangume masengwe ku masu

A child who did not listen grew horns on his forehead

Expl: There is a Tonga tale which says that a certain animal asked for horns to be on its forehead. When a drought came, this animal found it difficult to compete for water from a steep well. The tale teaches people to heed other people's advice.

Meaning: A person who does not follow other peoples' advice runs into trouble.

Occasion: Used to rebuke people when they get into trouble as a result of their selfish and self-centered behaviour. The proverb is also cited in a court setting to reprimand lawbreakers or disobedient children who are involved in a problem.

Related Biblical Themes and Stories:

1) "Arrogance causes nothing but trouble. It is wiser to ask advice" (*Proverbs 13:10*).

2) "Listen, my son, be wise and give serious thought to the way you live" (*Proverbs 23:19*).

3) "Listen to your father; without him you would not exist" (*Proverbs 23:22a*).

109. Mwana wamunyako ndi samba m'manja, wako ndi ryangako

Your neighbour's child is told, "Wash your hands"; yours is told, "You eat"

Expl: The treatment we give to our own children is often different from that given to other people's children. This results in mistreatment by some people of children put under their guardianship.

Meaning: It is not good to discriminate against other people's children who are in your care.

Occasion: Used to ridicule those who favour their own children in the home at the expense of those entrusted to them by relatives. It is therefore a warning to those who care for others in the extended family system.

Related Biblical Themes and Stories:

1) This proverb has the same principle as stipulated in the second most important biblical commandment: "Love your neighbour as you love yourself" (*Mark 12:31*).

110. Mwana wangu wakana marangu yiku yimulange ndi Njovu

If the child refuses to obey the rules, take him/her to the elephant to be punished

Expl: Without following rules, it is difficult for a child to acquire good moral standards or behave properly. The proverb is used metaphorically. The elephant is the most fearful and powerful animal.

Meaning: Children should not despise or disobey rules given by their parents or elders.

Occasion: This proverb addresses the theme of disobedience to the law. It is cited to warn those children who cannot heed advice from parents or elders.

Related Biblical Themes and Stories:

1) If the people disobeyed and did not faithfully keep God's rules and laws, many evil things would happen to them, and God would curse them (*Deuteronomy 28:15-19*).

2) If you get more stubborn every time you are corrected, one day you will be crushed and never recover (*Proverbs 29:1*).

3) In the history of Israel as God's people, when they disobeyed God's laws, they were punished by other nations from time to time. "In that day the Lord will whistle for the fly which is at the sources of the streams of Egypt and for the bee which is in the land of Assyria" (*Isaiah 7:18* RSV).

4) "You will not escape, you will be captured and handed over to him. You will see him face to face and talk to him in person; then you will go to Babylon" (*Jeremiah 34:3*).

Proveb 110: Mwana wangu wakana marangu yiku yimulange ndi Njovu
(If the child refuses to obey the rules, take him/her to the elephant to be punished)

111. Mweniyo wakwamphuwa kamunyake, kake nayo kakwamphuri-kenge

Anyone who takes away somebody's property, his or hers will also be taken away

Expl: People should not take away things that belong to others through violence, robbery and so on.

Meaning: A person should not covet somebody else's property. In other words, the strong should not look down on the weak.

Occasion: Used to warn people against practicing injustice. Everyone must be seen as equal before the law.

Related Biblical Themes and Stories:

1) The proverb illustrates David's situation in taking Uriah's wife. God did not let David's son from Uriah's wife live. David prayed to God that the child would get well. A week later the child died *(II Samuel 12:15-23)*.

2) For taking Uriah's wife and having Uriah killed, God said that he would cause a member of David's family to have intercourse with his wives in broad daylight *(II Samuel 12:1-12; 16:20-22)*.

3) In the parable of the unforgiving servant, the king was very angry and he sent the servant to jail to be punished until he should pay back the whole amount. This was because the servant himself ill-treated his friends *(Matthew 18:32-34)*.

112. Mzimu ndirinde

Take my hand, my ancestral spirit

Expl: The Tonga people believe that there are certain places which are inhabited by spirits: some good, others bad. These places are river valleys or river gorges and mountains.

Meaning: A shadow of death.

Occasion: Used when a person is travelling through dangerous places believed to be inhabited by the evil spirits, e.g., crossing river-gorges, passing through slopes of mountains or hills or passing through thick forests. It is used to give people courage because there is a power that protects them. Preachers use it to give hope to people that they are always with God who protects them.

Related Biblical Themes and Stories:

1) "Even if I go through the deepest darkness I will not be afraid, Lord, for you are with me. Your shepherd's rod and staff protect me" (*Psalm 23:4*).

2) "The danger of death was all around me; the horrors of the grave close in on me; I was filled with fear and anxiety. Then I called to the Lord, 'I beg you, Lord, save me!'" (*Psalm 116:3-4*).

3) "Let gloom and deep darkness claim it. Let clouds dwell upon it; let the blackness of the day terrify it" (*Job 3:5*).

113. Mzinda unyenga

A crowd cheats

Expl: It is not always true that the majority is on the right track or makes the correct decision. The minority can have bright ideas.

Meaning: A person should be cautious of what is said at gatherings.

Occasion: Sometimes cited to warn newly married people against acquiring bad influences from their peer groups that may spoil their marriage. It is also used by politicians when campaigning for their parties, perhaps challenging the views of the majority party in the current government. Also young people are advised to be analytical in their treatment of all that they hear at meetings with their peers.

Related Biblical Themes and Stories:

1) Don't be envious of evil people, and don't try to make friends with them. Causing trouble is all they ever think about; every time they open their mouth someone is going to be hurt (*Proverbs 24:1*).

2) The proverb can be related to the story of Paul sailing to Rome when there appeared a great storm at sea. Paul gave the people some advice, "Men I see that our voyage from here on will be dangerous; there will be great damage to the cargo and to the ship, and loss of life as well." But the army officer was convinced by what the captain and the owner of the ship (i.e., the majority) said (*Acts. 27:10-11*). Paul proved this afterwards when he stood before them (the majority) and said, "Men, you should have listened to me and not have sailed from Crete; then we should have avoided all this damage and loss" (*Acts. 27:21*).

115. Ndakana Chiuta mkali

I swear in the name of the angry God

Expl: This is a common Tonga way of using the name of *Chiuta* (God) in swearing or cursing. God is associated with lightning, so He is an angry God.

Meaning: An emphatic denial of guilt, implying a challenge to God to take revenge on a person if he/she is in the wrong.

Occasion: Used when a person wants to defend himself/herself in a court, i.e., to prove his/her innocence in the alleged matter. It is commonly used in families when something is stolen. Those concerned use the proverb implying that God will prove them innocent.

Related Biblical Themes and Stories:

1) "Everyone will come and kneel before me and swear to be loyal to me" (*Isaiah 45:23*).

2) Anyone in the land who asks for a blessing will ask to be blessed by the faithful God. Whoever takes an oath will swear by the name of the faithful God. The troubles of the past will be gone and forgotten (*Isaiah 65:16*).

116. Ndakukambiyanga kuti ndi Nyanga cha kweni mheni ndi tiringanenge

I told you that the cause was not witchcraft, but the one with whom you dip into the same plate

Expl: There are people who believe that suffering is caused by witchcraft.

Meaning: The person you trust most is the one who can harm you. Bad company spoils good character.

Occasion: Cited to warn young people who join bad company. They put much trust in some of their close friends, yet they forget that these very people can ruin their good behaviour or even cause them perpetual suffering.

Related Biblical Themes and Stories:

1) In the story about Paul's sufferings, those who stirred up people were his fellow Jews. In Lystra, some Jews came from Antioch in Pisidia and

from Iconium. They won the crowds and dragged Paul out of the town, thinking that he was dead (*Acts 14: 19-20*).

2) The Jews were jealous and gathered some of the worthless loafers from the streets and from a mob to attack the place where Paul and Silas were accommodated (*Acts 17:5*).

3) "Don't be envious of evil people, and don't try to make friends with them. Causing trouble is all they ever think about; every time they open their mouth someone is going to be hurt" (*Proverbs 24:1-2*).

4) "But look! The one who betrays me is here at the table with me" (*Luke 22:21*). Even the one who betrayed our Lord Jesus was a close friend.

117. Ndendengi waka ndi charu nde munthu na!

I shall be a wanderer on earth, because I am a person

Expl: The picture here is that of a nomad who has no permanent home and travels from place to place seeking rest.

Meaning: A person who is homeless or a wanderer.

Occasion: Cited by a person who has no one to help him/her, and who has no permanent settlement.

Related Biblical Themes and Stories:

1) "I will be a homeless wanderer on the earth and anyone who finds me will kill me" (Genesis 4:12-14).

2) "It was faith that made Abraham obey when God called him to go out to a country which God had promised to give him. He left his own country without knowing where he was going" *(Hebrews 11:8).*

118. Ndiruta kwa ama ungandipweteka

I am going back to my mother lest you hurt me

Expl: It is usual for wives who are maltreated to go back to their mothers.

Meaning: You should not tolerate a husband who mistreats you too much. Otherwise you lose your dignity.

Occasion: The proverb addresses the theme of self-respect. It is cited in families where husband and wife do not live a peaceful life.

Related Biblical Themes and Stories:

1) When the prodigal son realized that his dignity was lost, he, at last came to his senses and said, "All my father's hired workers have more than they can eat, and here I am about to starve! I will get up and go to my father and say, father, I have sinned against God and against you" *(Luke 15:17)*.

119. Ndarama zapa mutu

The money on the head

Expl: In an informal Tonga marriage, the husband owes his wife's people damages plus an unspecified bridewealth. When the husband has paid the damages, his in-laws will mention the remaining amount of bridewealth.

Meaning: The money paid for seducing a woman.

Occasion: Used in court when a person is convicted in a case where he was found committing adultery. The payment to the woman's parents is referred to as 'the money on the head' or the money for adultery.

Related Biblical Themes and Stories:

1) This proverb reflects the story about Abraham and Abimelech. Although in a dream Abimelech was warned by God not to do anything evil to Sarah, the concept of giving gifts to Abraham affirms a similar idea in this proverb. "Then Abimelech gave Sarah back to Abraham, and at the same time he gave him sheep, cattle, slaves, some land and money" *(Genesis 20:4-18)*.

2) In Jewish custom, if a man rapes a girl who is not engaged, he is fined a bride price and made to marry the girl, whom he cannot divorce *(Deuteronomy 22:28-29)*.

120. Ng'ombe yo yadanjiya yitumwa maji ghakutowa

The first cow drinks clean water

Expl: The Tonga people are known as adventurous in all walks of life. People should go into new ventures whose markets are still virtually untapped, rather than into ones where markets are almost flooded with goods. The English proverb equivalent to this is, "The early bird catches the worm."

Meaning: A person who starts something such as a business earlier usually succeeds.

Occasion: Used to encourage young people who want to undertake something to do so before others do. Also, when advising farmers that a bumper crop can only be realized if one starts planting in the early rains.

Related Biblical Themes and Stories:

1) The concept drawn out from the proverb is that of a race or people in a competition. As Paul puts it to the Philippians: "Of course, my brothers, I really do not think that I have already won it, the one thing I do, however, is to forget what is behind me and do my best to reach what is ahead" (*Philippians 3:13*).

2) "Every morning each one gathered as much as he needed; and when the sun grew hot, what was left on the ground melted" (*Exodus 16:21*).

121. Njovu yitufwa ndi mivwi yinande

An elephant dies because of many arrows

Expl: The Tonga people believe in communal work. You need many shots to kill an elephant. The English equivalent is, "Many hands make light work." The proverb is used metaphorically.

Meaning: A big task or problem can only be accomplished or solved by many people.

Occasion: Used when advising a person to call upon others to come to his/her aid. Usually the proverb is used during harvesting time when more labour or support effort is needed. Christians use it to encourage people to work together on church projects.

Related Biblical Themes and Stories:

1) "No one can break into a strong man's house and take away his belongings unless he first ties up the strong man; then he can plunder his house" (*Mark 3:27*).

Poverb 120: Ng'ombe yo yadanjiya yatumwa maji ghakutowa
(The first cow drinks clean water)

2) "Be brave, Philistines, fight like men, or we will become slaves to the Hebrews, just as they were our slaves. So fight like men" (*I Samuel 4:9*).

3) "Finally, build up your strength in union with the Lord and by means of his mighty power. Put on all the armor that God gives you, so that you will be able to stand up against the Devil's evil tricks" (*Ephesians 6:10-20*).

4) "So Ruth went out to the fields and walked behind the workers, picking up the heads of grain which they left" (*Ruth 2:3*).

122. Njuchi yo yakuruma ndiyo yako

A bee that stings you is yours

Expl: When a person has a problem, she/he asks someone whom she/he trusts will come to her/his aid. The analogy gives a picture of a swarm of bees; one bee leaves all others to sting a person.

Meaning: A person asks for help from his relatives or close friends.

Occasion: Cited when a request is made by a person involved in a problem. It is used to encourage inter-dependence.

Related Biblical Themes and Stories:

1) Rachel ran to tell her father, and when he heard the news about his nephew Jacob, he ran to meet him, hugged him and kissed him, and brought him into the house. When Jacob told Laban everything that had happened, Laban said, "Yes, indeed you are my own flesh and blood." Jacob stayed there a whole month *(Genesis 29:9-14)*.

2) Moses escaped from Egypt to the land of the Midianites, where he was received by Jethro, the priest of Midian. Jethro asked his daughters, "Why did you leave the man out there? Go and invite him to eat with us." So Moses decided to live there, and Jethro gave him his daughter Zipporah in marriage *(Exodus 2:16-22)*.

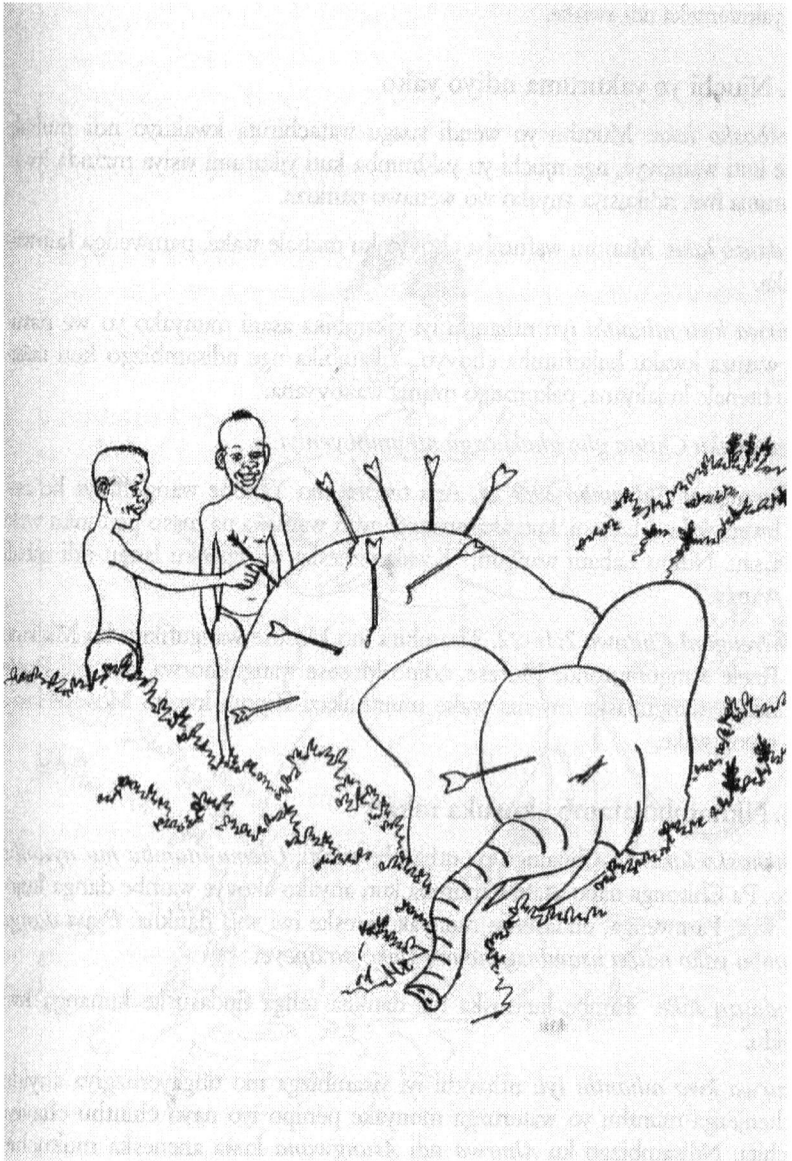

Proverb 121: Njovu yitufwa ndi mivwi yinande
(An elephant dies because of many arrows)

123. Nkhombo atamba kusuka mkati

A calabash is first cleaned from the inside

Expl: The proverb is the equivalent of the English saying, "Charity begins at home." A person should put his/her house in order before he/she can tell others to do the same.

Meaning: We should not blame our friends before we check on ourselves.

Occasion: It is told to show disregard when everyone knows the person giving advice has not followed it himself. It also teaches young people to be honest with themselves.

Related Biblical Themes and Stories:

The proverb is related to the theme of judging others. For instance, Jesus advised his hearers not to judge others, so that God will not judge them. He said, "God will judge you in the same way you judge others, and he will apply to you the same rules you apply to others. Why, then, do you look at the speck in you brother's eye and pay no attention to the log in you own eye? How dare you say to your brother, "Please let me take that speck out of your eye when you have a log in your own eye. You hypocrite! First take the log out of your own eye, and then you will be able to see clearly to take the speck out of your brother's eye" (Matthew 7:1-5).

124. Nkhondo ndi mnasi

The one who starts war against you is your neighbour

Expl: It is a relative who in many cases stirs up troubles. It is a relative who can easily ruin or end your life.

Meaning: A person you trust is the one who destroys you.

Occasion: Used to warn a person against trusting someone who in turn might plot against one.

Related Biblical Themes and Stories:

1) Absalom plotted against his father, King David. The plot against the King gained strength, and Absalom's followers grew in numbers *(II Samuel 15:9-12)*.

2) Judas Iscariot betrayed Jesus, his master *(Mark 14:17-20, 43-44)*.

Proverb 123: Nkhombo atamba kusuka mkati
(A calabash is first cleaned from the inside)

125. Nkhuni yimoza yimanga chifinga cha

One piece of firewood does not make a fire

Expl: A person is valued for what he/she is able to contribute to society.

Meaning: We need to cooperate with others. No man is an island unto himself.

Occasion: The proverb addresses the need for unity in a community. It is cited to warn people against practicing individualism. They should learn to bear one another's burdens. Preachers can use it to encourage Christian fellowship.

Related Biblical Themes and Stories:

1) "How wonderful it is, how pleasant, for God's people to live together in harmony!" *(Psalm 133:1)*.

2) "For where two or three come together in my name, I am there with them" *(Matthew 18:20)*.

3) "Help to carry one another's burdens" *(Galatians 6:2)*.

4) "Let us not give up the habit of meeting together, as some are doing. Instead let us encourage one another" *(Hebrews 10:25)*.

126. Nkhurande zibaya Njovu

Red ants kill an elephant

Expl: A problem can be solved more effectively and efficiently by people working together. Although ants are small, they are clever and united.

Meaning: People with common interests, abilities, and natures usually do great things together.

Occasion: Used to advise people of the same clan or other recognized group who are not approaching each other for assistance. People who cooperate share their knowledge in solving problems.

Related Biblical Themes and Stories:

1) "People learn from one another, just as iron sharpens iron" *(Proverbs 27:17)*.

2. "Ants: they are weak, but they store up their food in the summer" *(Proverbs 30:25)*.

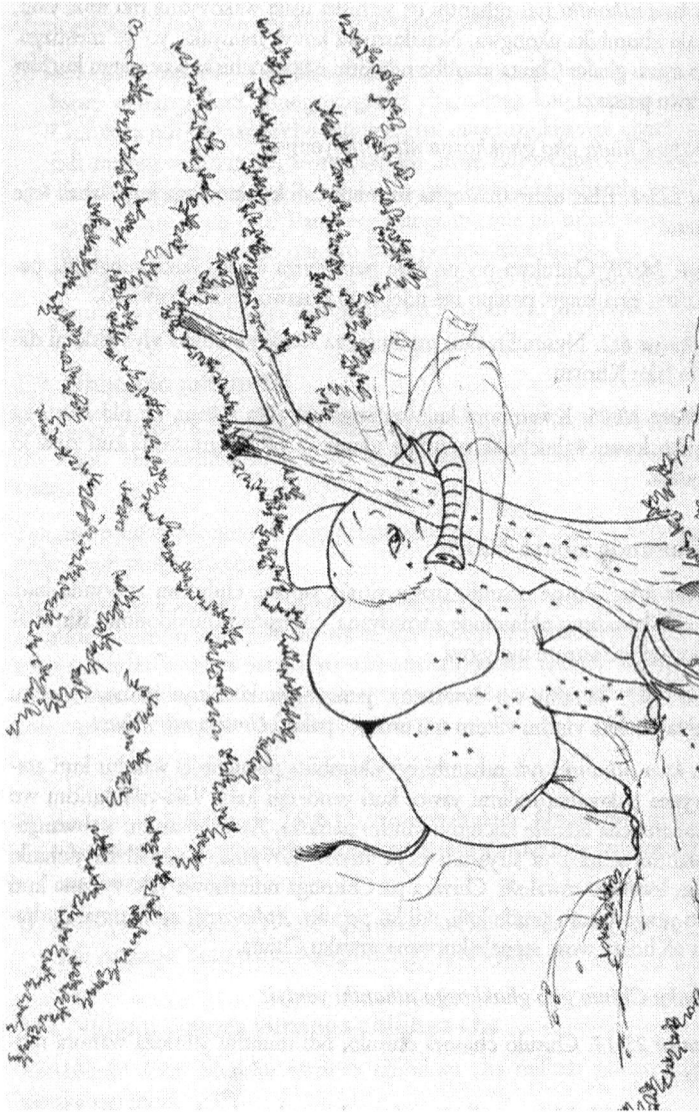

Proverb 126: Nkhurande zibaya njovu
(Red ants kill an elephant)

127. Nozga kapasi mwakuti kapachanya kasike

Take care of that which is down, so that the one which is still up does not come down

Expl: Things that are properly done or planned have good results. It is similar to the English proverb: "A good beginning makes a good ending." We should take care of little things which may bear implications for greater things.

Meaning: Doing things well earns one greater trust. The implication is similar again to an English proverb: "Charity begins at home."

Occasion: It is told when advising someone to manage his/her responsibilities properly in order to be trusted and possibly earn himself a promotion or many followers. One must take the initiative so that something better can be done. Often young people are advised to lay a good foundation for their bright future, e.g., concentrating in school.

Related Biblical Themes and Stories:

1) Paul reminds the Philippians to take some initiative in working out their salvation. What comes from above is a fulfillment. "Keep on working with fear and trembling to complete your salvation" (*Philippians 2:12*).

2) Likewise the prophet Isaiah advised King Hezekiah to put everything in order before he died: "The Lord tells you that you are to put everything in order because you will not recover, get ready to die (*Isaiah 38:1*).

128. Nthengwa ya ubwezi

A marriage of friendship

Expl: The Tonga describe a marriage as "formal" or "informal." In the case of the "informal," the man simply brings gifts to the woman without really committing himself to the payment of bridewealth (*chilowola*).

Meaning: A marriage where no bridewealth is paid to the wife's people.

Occasion: Used to ridicule a young woman who has been cheated with gifts given by a man who in the end might not even marry her. Such a marriage is adulterous and is regarded as a marriage of the bush, as opposed to an acceptable marriage where bridewealth is paid. Preachers always use the proverb to condemn marriages which are not Christian and not built upon Christian teachings.

Related Biblical Themes and Stories:

1) When Abraham's servant asked for the hand of Rebecca to be married to Isaac, "he brought out clothing and silver and gold jewelry, and gave them to Rebecca. He also gave expensive gifts to her brother and to her mother" *(Genesis 24:53).*

2) David sent messengers to get Bathsheba. They brought her to him and he made love to her *(II Samuel 11:4).*

3) "How hard it is to find a capable wife! She is worth far more than jewels. Her husband puts his confidence in her" *(Proverbs 31:10-11).*

4) "A married woman is bound by the law to her husband" *(Romans 7:2).*

129. Nyifwa nkhungona

Death is sleep

Expl: Death is referred to as sleep. It is the belief that people who die will one day be raised from the dead.

Meaning: Death is not the end of a person's life.

Occasion: Used to show courage in the face of death. It is not the end of a person's life. Preachers have used it to exhort Christians that death is a way to the new life.

Related Biblical Themes and Stories:

1) Jesus referred to the death of Lazarus as sleep: "Our friend Lazarus has fallen asleep, but I go to awake him out of sleep" *(John 11:11* RSV).

2) "Those who have died believing will rise to life first" *(I Thessalonians 4:16).*

130. Nyifwa ye pose

Death is everywhere

Expl: We cannot escape death.

Meaning: Everyone will die.

Occasion: Cited as a reminder to people when a sudden death has occurred, such as death caused by accidents away from the deceased's homeland. Death can occur anywhere, any time. Most Christian preachers cite this proverb at funerals.

Related Biblical Themes and Stories:

1) "If I lay down in the world of the dead, you would be there" (*Psalm 139:8*).

2) "Sin came into the world through one man, and his sin brought death with it. As a result, death has spread to the whole human race because everyone has sinned" (*Romans 5:12*).

131. Nyoko ndi nyoko chingana wapunduki

Your mother is your mother even if she is disabled

Expl: It would not be possible to be born into the world without a mother.

Meaning: People should not disobey, disown or disregard their parents.

Occasion: Often used when reproaching children who are extremely rude and disobedient to their parents or elders, as well as those who are unkind and inconsiderate, even disowning their own parents.

Related Biblical Themes and Stories:
The proverb addresses the theme of obedience. It teaches obedience to parents and elders, as well as pride in one's parental background:

1) The Bible tells us to respect our fathers and mothers so that we may live a longer time (*Exodus 20:12*).

2) In Ephesians 6:3, children are advised to obey their parents, as part of their Christian duty, for it is the right thing to do so.

3) In Deuteronomy 27:16, God's curse is on anyone who dishonors his father or mother.

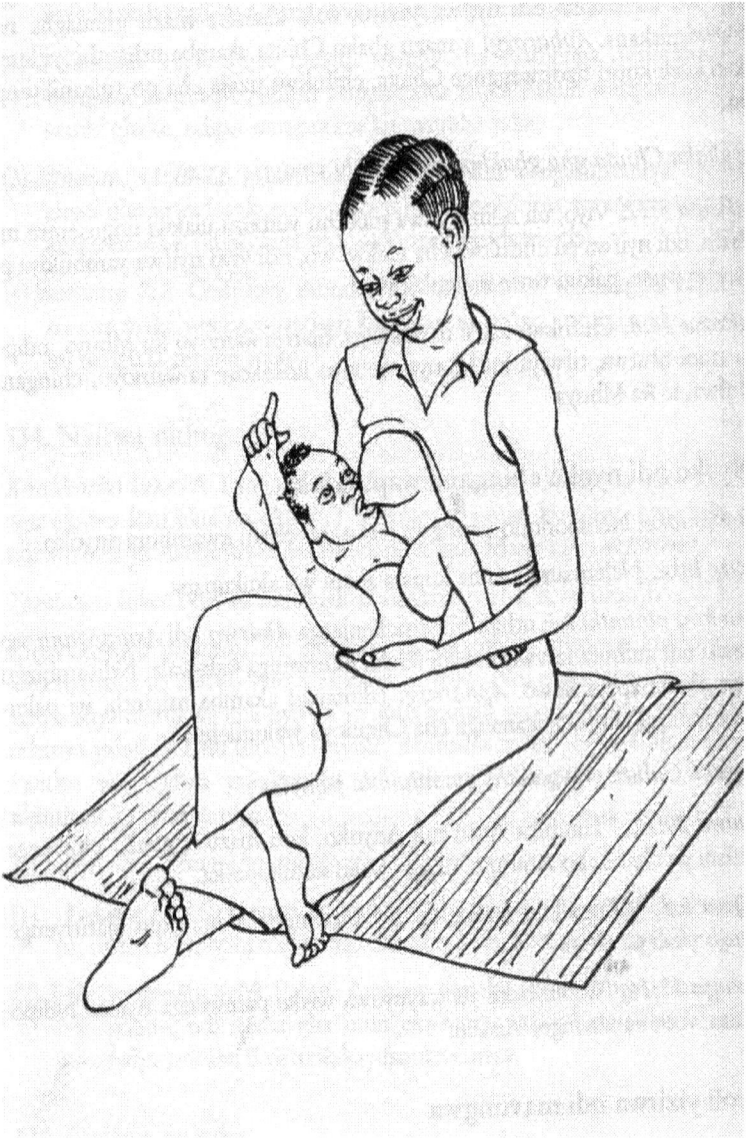

Proverb 131: Nyoko ndi nyoko chingana wapunduki
(Your mother is your mother even if she is disabled)

132. Nyoli yizirwa ndi mavungwa

A chicken is dignified by feathers

Expl: Tonga people believe that a person is more respected if he/she has children. Thus a condition for a permanent marriage is the provision of children.

Meaning: An old person is respected because of his/her children.

Occasion: Cited when urging a young person whose wife or husband is believed to have failed to bear children to marry another one in the hope that this may help him bear some children.

Related Biblical Themes and Stories:

The proverb is related to what Jesus said to his disciples. A Christian can only be dignified if he/she is in Christ and only then can bear good fruits. Jesus said, "I am the real vine and my Father is the gardener. He breaks off every branch in my that does not bear more fruit. You have been made clean already by the teaching I have given you., Remain united to me and I will remain united to you. A branch cannot bear fruit itself; it can do so only if it remains in the vine. In the same way you cannot bear fruit unless you remain in me"(John 15:1-5).

133. Palima mpha moyo

What cultivates is the stomach

Expl: The proverb is used metaphorically to indicate that a person who is hungry cannot work, but one who has eaten some food has the energy to work.

Meaning: Food gives energy to a person.

Occasion: Used when advising a wife to prepare food for a husband if she expects him to do a good job at the garden.

Related Biblical Themes and Stories:

1) Jesus said, "I was hungry and you fed me" (*Matthew 25:35*).

2) The disciples of Jesus saw that the crowd was hungry and could withstand no longer to hear the Word of God. They asked Jesus to send them away in order to buy something to eat. In the end Jesus fed the people (*Mark 6:36-44*).

3) Jesus felt sorry for the hungry people, fearing they would faint as they left. Jesus fed them. Everybody ate and had enough (*Mark 8:2-9*).

4) Since food gives energy, after healing Jairus's daughter, Jesus said, "Give her something to eat" (*Mark 5:43*).

134. Panyifwa yangu fuvu lazamtenje

At my death, dust shall mourn

Expl: The proverb shows the concerns that Tonga people have about death. Death causes many people to suffer, especially the dependents of the deceased.

Meaning: The death of someone upon whom many relatives depend is a great loss.

Occasion: Cited at the funeral of an important person such as a Chief or other important figure in a community. Sometimes it is cited by a person who is responsible for the welfare of others as his/her last word uttered on the deathbed. The implication is that after the death, there will be much suffering and wailing.

Related Biblical Themes and Stories:

1) The proverb draws the picture of Jesus' entry into Jerusalem when he said, "I tell you, if these keep silent, the very stones would cry out" *(Luke 19:40).*

2) "Daughters of Jerusalem, do not weep for me, but weep for yourselves and for your children" *(Luke 23:28).*

3) "I know that after I leave, fierce wolves will come among you and they will not spare the flock. Watch, then" *(Acts 20:29-31).*

135. Pepa, pepa

Be appeased, be appeased

Expl: The proverb was repeated as an act of worship in homage to the dead, while people would clap their hands as a gesture of salutation.

Meaning: An address for appeasement, given to the dead as a last respect.

the people laid the corpse in the grave, the friends gathered around the open grave. The request is made so that the spirit of the dead person may go away to the spirit land and let alone the living.

Related Biblical Themes and Stories:

1) "A man may have a hundred children and live a long time, but no matter how long he lives, if he does not get his share of happiness and does not receive a decent burial, then I say that a baby born dead is better off" *(Ecclesiastes 6:3).*

2) "What she did was to pour this perfume on my body to get me ready for burial" *(Matthew 26:12).*

Occasion: Commonly cited at a funeral gathering to show concern about the loss of a beloved one. In the olden times, it was cited during burial. Before

Proverb 135: Pepa pepa
(Be appeased, be appeased)

136. Po pasamba msambazi ndipo patumwa mkavu

Where the rich person bathes, there also the poor drink

Expl: The marginalised, poor and disadvantaged in Tonga society often ask help from the well-to-do person.

Meaning: We should share what we have with the needy.

Occasion: Used when advising the well-to-do people to help those who are disadvantaged, poor or marginalised in the society. The things we require for our welfare are the same things they require. Therefore, sharing with them is what should be encouraged. Christians are exhorted by the preachers to help one another.

Related Biblical Themes and Stories:

1) The proverb is affirmed by the story about the rich man and Lazarus: "There was also a poor man named Lazarus, covered with sores, who used to be brought to the rich man's door", *(Luke 16:20).*

2) "Share your belongings with your needy fellow Christians and open your house to strangers" *(Romans 12:13).*

137. Po paswela Kambwe pe nkhulande

Where the fox delays, there are ants

Expl: There is always some reason if a person stops at a particular place or frequents a place.

Meaning: When a person frequents a place, she/he is bound to be accused of committing some offense.

Occasion: Used to warn a person against associating himself/herself with a place which is likely to invite trouble for him/her. Boys in particular are advised not to visit places where they are likely to meet girls and be accused of fornication.

Related Biblical Themes and Stories:

1) "Wherever there is a dead body, the vultures will gather" *(Matthew 24:28).*

2) "Avoid immorality" *(I Corinthians 6:18).*

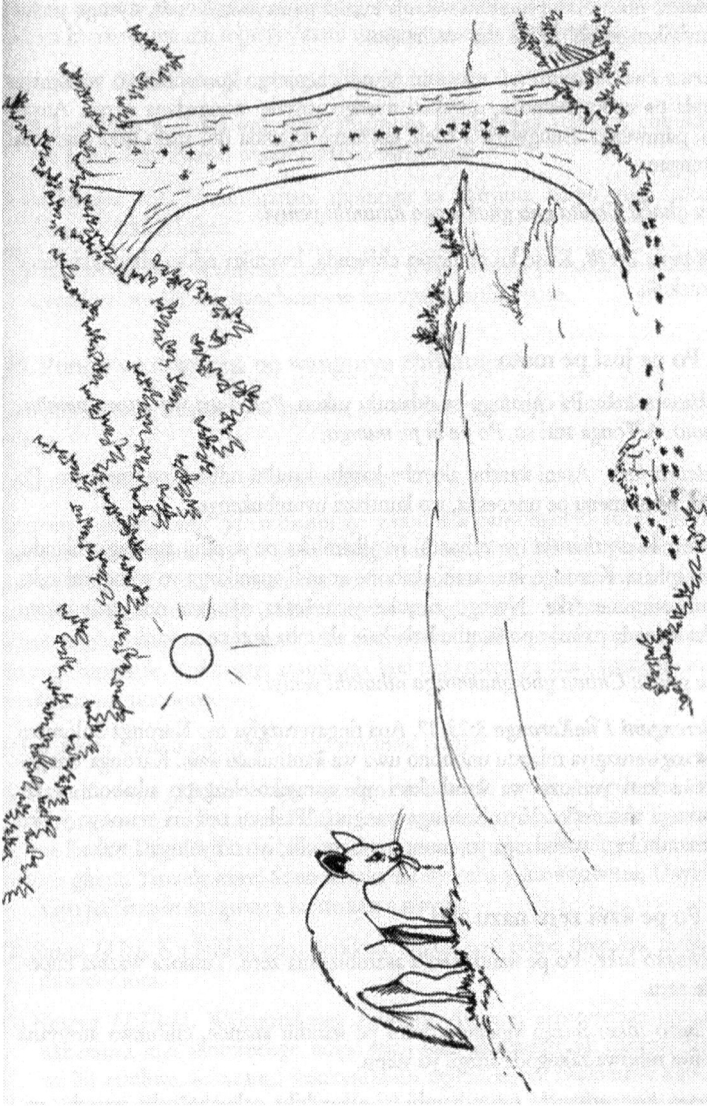

Proverb 137: Popasweta kambwe pe nkhurande
(Where the folks delays there are ants

138. Po pe josi pe moto

Where smoke is coming from, there is fire

Expl: The equivalent English proverb is, "There is no smoke without fire." Rumours often are found to be true.

Meaning: There is some truth in anything that many constantly talk about.

Occasion: Used in a court setting to show the judges' feeling that a statement or crime, though denied by one of the parties in the case, has some truth because of the many people who testify about it. It is also used to advise young people to avoid places where elders say there may be danger.

Related Biblical Themes and Stories:

The proverb can be related to the story of Solomon judging a difficult case between the two women. King Solomon believed that one of these women told the truth. "Then King Solomon said, 'Each of you claims that the living child is hers and that the dead child belongs to the other one.' He sent for a sword and when it was brought he said, 'Cut the living child in two and give each woman half of it.' The real mother, her heart full of love for her son said to the King, 'Please your Majesty, don't kill the child! Give it to her!' But the other woman said, 'Don't give it to either of us, go on and cut it in two.' Then Solomon said, 'Don't kill the child! Give it to the first woman— she is its real mother'" (*I Kings 3:23-27*).

139. Po pe wawi zeru nazu ziwi

Where there are two people, wisdom is two

Expl: Where there are two people, there is double wisdom.

Meaning: A problem can be better solved by more than one person.

Occasion: Cited to advise a person who is trying to solve a problem all by himself/herself and fails. It can also be used to encourage people to solve problems together. It is therefore cited to teach the value of cooperation and inter-dependence.

Related Biblical Themes and Stories:

1) Two are better off than one, because together they can work more effec- tively *(Ecclesiastes 4:9).*

2) "The spirit's presence is shown in some way in each person for the good of all" *(I Corinthians 12:7).*

3) "Help to carry one another's burdens" *(Galatians 6:2)*.

140. Pundu waruwa cha po wangurya chiwanga

A hyena never forgets where he ate a bone

Expl: A person does not forget the one who renders help. That is, the person making the request is appreciative of the previous help rendered.

Meaning: A person normally seeks help from one who assisted him previously.

Occasion: The proverb is used by a person in need as an introduction to an intended request for further assistance from one who had previously assisted him. It is also used to remind those ungrateful people who, as soon as things go well, despise those who helped them out of difficulty. They forget that someday they will need to go back to the same person when they need more help. Young people are warned against despising the places or people who brought them up.

Related Biblical Themes and Stories:

1) This proverb reflects the message of Hosea. Israel becomes apostate, but in the end returns to her God. The story of Gomer and Hosea illustrated this point *(Hosea 3; 6:1)*. Thus, Israel will come back to the Lord for protection: "My people will follow me when I roar like a Lion at their enemies. They will hurry to me from the west. They will come from Egypt, as swiftly as birds, and from Assyria, like doves. I will bring them to their homes again" *(Hosea 11:10-11)*.

2) "What portion have we in David? We have no inheritance in the son of Jesse. To your tents, O Israel! Look now to your own house, David" *(I Kings 12:16)*. This picture of a divided Kingdom reflects the idea in the proverb that the people do not forget places of peace and tranquillity.

3) "By the waters of Babylon, there we sat down and wept, when we remembered Zion" *(Psalm 137:1)*.

141. Pusi wakukota atimuliska wana wake

When a monkey becomes old, it is fed by its young ones

Expl: An old monkey cannot have the strength to find its own food. It needs energy to jump from each branch of the tree to another. Therefore, its young ones feed it.

Meaning: People should look after their aged parents and relatives.

Occasion: Cited to advise a carefree young person to take care of needy parents or relatives. In so doing, they show their respect to them.

Related Biblical Themes and Stories:

The proverb addresses caring for others. The story of Jacob and Esau reflects this point. Isaac said, "You see that I am old and may die soon. Take your bow and arrows, go out into the country and kill an animal for me, cook me some of that tasty food that I like and bring it to me. After I have eaten it, I will give you my final blessing before I die" (*Genesis 27:2-4*).

Proverb 141: Pusi wakukota atimuliska wana wake
(When a monkey becomes old, it is fed by its young ones)

142. Rekani kuruta nayo Chiuta waje penepano

Don't go away with your God, he should stay here

Expl: The saying reflects the people's belief that the early missionaries brought their God to them. It originates from a legend that when the missionaries left a place, it was believed that they carried their God away.

Meaning: Other people or races will believe in God.

Occasion: Generally cited after a big evangelical meeting that touched the hearts of the people. The charismatic power manifested in some early missionaries convinced the local people that these missionaries had a God with them.

Related Biblical Themes and Stories:

1) Laban had gone to shear his sheep, and during his absence Rachel stole the household gods that belonged to her father *(Genesis 31:19).*

2) "Naaman said, 'Now I know that there is no god but the God of Israel; so please, sir, accept a gift from me'" *(II Kings 5:15).*

143. Somba yakuvunda pamphika yiziwa kuvundiska zose

One rotten fish in the pot can make all other good fish rot also

Expl: A small mistake a person makes can affect not only himself/herself but also others.

Meaning: One bad individual can spoil others.

Occasion: Cited to warn a person about joining bad company that might spoil his/her good behaviour. It is also used as advice to people who are in charge of others to see that they do not employ troublemakers who can mislead others in a working community.

Related Biblical Themes and Stories:

1) "Keep company with the wise and you will become wise. If you make friends with stupid people you will be ruined" *(Proverbs 13:20).*

144. Sonu awiya ose pa msana pe, ndikuti manja pu! pu! Pepa, pepa

Then they all fall over onto their backs assenting by clapping their hands and saying, "Be appeased, be appeased"

Expl: This is a proverbial prayer in Tonga traditional religion. It is a request that the spirit should go away to the spirit-land and leave the living or, if it continues to interfere in their affairs, that the spirit might work only for the good of its friends and relations, and provide them with abundance of the desirable things of life.

Occasion: Used at traditional worship, when offering sacrifices to the ancestors as one way of appeasing them or seeking their favour.

Related Biblical Themes and Stories:

1) "Receive my prayer as incense, my uplifted hands as an evening sacrifice" (*Psalm 141:2*).

2) "Make an altar of earth for me and on it sacrifice your sheep and your cattle as offerings to be completely burned and as peace offerings. In every place that I set aside for you to worship me, I will come to you and bless you" (*Exodus 20:24*).

3) "And this is the Law of the sacrifice of peace offerings which one may offer to the Lord." (*Leviticus 7:11-13*).

145. Sunga khose mukanda wazamuvwara

Keep your neck, you will wear the beads

Expl: There are good things in store for a person, so one should be careful with one's life. If you want to enjoy good things, do not become impatient.

Meaning: A person should obey the rules given to him/her.

Occasion: Cited to advise young people who think they can have things before they are ready for them. For instance, students are advised to obey certain rules at school (e.g., follow study times, work hard, etc.), in order to prepare for their successful future. Young people should also obey the rules given by their parents. It can be used to exhort people to be patient with their lives.

Related Biblical Themes and Stories:

1) "Poor and humble people will once again find the happiness which the Lord, the Holy God of Israel gives" (*Isaiah 29:19*).

2) "Blessed are the meek, for they shall inherit the earth" (*Matthew 5:5*).

3) "Sons, listen to what your father teaches you. Pay attention, and you will have understanding" (*Proverbs 4:1*).

4) "Son, do what your father tells you and never forget what your mother taught you. Their teaching will lead you when you travel, protect you at night" (*Proverbs 6:20-24*).

146. Sunga phazi lako ko utenda

Keep your feet wherever you travel

Expl: People should maintain good morals wherever they might be.

Meaning: A person should be careful with what he/she says in public.

Occasion: Used when advising a person to avoid indulging in immoral practices which can spoil one's name. Preachers can use it to exhort Christians to live lives that glorify God.

Related Biblical Themes and Stories:

1) "Guard your steps when you go to the house of God; to draw near to listen is better than to offer the sacrifice of fools; for they do not know that they are doing evil" *(Ecclesiastes 5:1* RSV*)*.

2) "Even the dust from your town that sticks to our feet we wipe off against you" *(Luke 10:11)*.

3) "So be careful how you live" *(Ephesians 5:5)*.

4) "Whatever you do, whether you eat or drink, do it all for God's glory. Live in such a way as to cause no trouble either to Jews or Gentiles or to the church" *(I Corinthians 10:31-32)*.

147. Te waranda

We are forsaken

Expl: Malanda in Tonga means "orphan." When the people have no rains, they have no food. In a way they are forsaken or orphaned. The word

Mlanda is sometimes used for people of all ages who have lost their biological parents. They need protection and care.

Meaning: People appear to be destitute while the rain refuses to come, because they have no food.

Occasion: Chanted as part of a rain prayer. Preachers also use it when presenting the people's needs to God, who is the provider of good things to his destitute people.

Related Biblical Themes and Stories:

1) "I will be with you; I will not fail you or forsake you" *(Joshua 1:5* RSV*)*.

2) "You have been my help; don't abandon me, O God, my savior" *(Psalm 27:9)*.

3) "My God, my God, why hast thou forsaken me?" *(Mark 15:34* RSV*)*.

148. Tilakata nge maluwa

We fall away like flowers

Expl: Death is very common in Tonga society—especially these days when many deaths occur because of AIDS. The picture is that life withers like flowers.

Meaning: The life of a person is temporary.

Occasion: Used as a lament over the untimely deaths which occur from time to time in our communities. Preachers use the proverb to warn the people against being careless with their lives. Life withers like flowers which appear healthy and beautiful in the morning but wither away in the evening. Preachers also use it to advise Christians that the life they have belongs to God. He can take it at anytime.

Related Biblical Themes and Stories:

1) "As for us our life is like grass. We grow and flourish like a wild flower; then the wind blows on it and it is gone" *(Psalm 103:15-16)*.

2) "All mankind are like grass, and all their glory is like wild flowers. The grass withers, and the flowers fall" *(I Peter 1:24; Isaiah 40:6-8)*.

149. Tiruta msana wale—kurondo anyido

We are leaving today—we follow our fellows

Expl: In Tonga tradition, before the *Azukuru* (those who dress the corpse) take the corpse away, they chant this proverb. It is a declaration that the burial will be performed on that day.

Meaning: We are now taking the dead body for burial.

Occasion: Cited by the *Azukuru* on a burial day. Preachers can use it to warn people to prepare for death and the Lord's return.

Related Biblical Themes and Stories:

1) "And Moses took the bones of Joseph with him; for Joseph had solemnly sworn to the people of Israel, saying, 'God will visit you; then you must carry my bones with you from here'" *(Exodus 13:19).*

2) "Man goes to his eternal home and the mourners go about the streets" *(Ecclesiastes 12:5).*

3) "Let the dead bury their own dead" *(Matthew 8:22).*

4) "And you, too, must be ready, because the Son of Man will come at an hour when you are not expecting him" *(Luke 12:40).*

150. Ubwezi ngwawaka kanthu mbubali

Kinship is better than friendship

Expl: The proverb originates from a Tonga tale in which a Chief abandoned all his relatives because of his friend. In the end, he discovered that his relatives were more valuable than his friend.

Meaning: Friendship lapses or ends, but not kinship.

Occasion: Used when warning a person against spending his/her wealth on a friend. When trouble comes, the friend may not care about him/her. It is also used to ridicule a person who spent all his wealth with friends and ends up poor. His friends begin to run away from him.

Related Biblical Themes and Stories:

1) "My close friends have failed me" *(Job 19:14* RSV).

2) "Even my best friend, the one I trusted most, the one who shared my food, has turned against me" *(Psalm 41:9).*

151. Ubwezi wa mbavi wambura kurumba mbuyaki

The friendship between an ax and its carrier

Expl: The person you help can turn against you next time.

Meaning: A person who does not appreciate something good done to him/her.

Occasion: Used to reprimand people who return evil to those who helped them. Such people have no appreciation whatsoever.

Related Biblical Themes and Stories:

1) The story about David and Saul can be a good example here. At first, Saul liked the young man, David (*I Samuel 16:21-22*).

2) But one day King Saul turned against David in order to kill him (*I Samuel 18:10-11*).

152. Uchiwinda ukamba wako

You should only talk of your own hunting skills

Expl: There is a common folktale. When Man and Lion became friends, both were hunters. Lion warned Man not to reveal his practices in the skills of hunting. Man eventually did not keep the secret. He revealed the activities of Lion, and Lion heard about it. In anger Lion quickly ran to Man's home village, where he killed the Chief's daughter. The allegation was that Man killed the Chief's daughter (that is, that Man's foolish action had angered Lion and led to the girl's death). This eventually led the Chief to kill him. Because Man had talked more of Lion's activities than his own, he lost his life.

Meaning: A person should mind his/her own business.

Occasion: Used to advise a person not to involve himself in other people's affairs. It is also cited to warn people to keep away from gossip. The proverb is also used to advise young people to keep secrets and promises so that they become reliable and responsible.

Related Biblical Themes and Stories:

The proverb addresses the theme of responsibility:

1) "Why then do you look at the speck in your brother's eye and pay no attention to the log in your own eye? How dare you say to your brother,

'Please, let me take that speck out of your eye.' You hypocrite! First take the log out of your own eye and then you will be able to see clearly to take the speck out of you brother's eye" (*Matthew 7:3-5*).

2) "Don't give evidence against someone else without good reason or say misleading things about him" (*Proverbs 24:28*).

153. Uku-vyanowa, uku-vyanowa, Pusi wanguwa chagada

This is sweet and that is also sweet! A monkey missed a branch and fell upside down

Expl: One must choose one thing at a time. A Tonga tale depicts a hyena who burst his stomach because he would not choose between two paths that both had delicious smells. He tried to follow both paths to the good smells but ended up by splitting himself open in the middle.

Meaning: A person who usually does wrong things will one day be caught.

Occasion: Used to advise young people to make wise decisions. Sometimes it is used when commenting on a person so caught; or when advising a person known to be indulging in some bad practices to stop. It is also a piece of advice for people who are greedy and corrupt. They should not think everything is theirs.

Related Biblical Themes and Stories:

1) The proverb can be related to the advice Jesus gave in the Sermon on the Mount. He said, "No one can be a slave of two masters, he will hate one and love the other. You cannot serve both God and money" (*Matthew 6:24*). Here we see one is to choose the right thing, and that is serving God. Money is a symbol of evil.

2) "He who is greedy for unjust gain makes trouble for his household" (*Proverbs 15:27*).

154. Ulemu ubaya

Kindness kills

Expl: The Tonga have several folktales which portray kindness as a way of inviting danger. For instance, when Kalulu (Hare) helps Snake to escape from a trap, Snake in turn wants to bite Hare. Thus the motif, "The good are not spared."

Meaning: Some people are ungrateful, i.e., they do not appreciate one's kindness.

Occasion: Normally used negatively when regretting a person's unbecoming deeds towards a friend or a neighbour. It is a warning to people to be careful with those who pose as friends, since people can pretend to be friendly at one time while they plan to do evil. Young people are warned against spending all their time with friends who are unreliable.

Related Biblical Themes and Stories:

1) The proverb is related to the kind deeds Jesus did, and each time he showed such kindness to people they plotted against his life. For instance, after Jesus raised Lazarus from the dead, the Jewish authorities planned to kill him (*John 11:53*).

2) In Lystra, Paul was stoned because of healing a crippled man (*Acts 14:1-19*).

3) In Philippi, Paul and Silas were arrested for healing a slave girl who had an evil spirit that enabled her to predict the future. She earned a lot of money by telling fortunes (*Acts. 1:16-24*).

155. Umoyo wamunthu ndi Chiuta

A person's life is God

Expl: This is a Tonga belief that man's source of life is God (*Chiuta*). God is thought of as a Spirit and not man; He is the Supreme Spirit.

Meaning: God is the one who protects every person's life.

Occasion: Cited to advise a person to take care of his/her life, because it belongs to God. Preachers often admonish people who live a careless life or who depend on themselves without putting their trust in God. It can be used to assure people of God's protection and deliverance from the hand of their enemies.

Related Biblical Themes and Stories:

1) "Then I called on the name of the Lord: 'O Lord, I beseech thee, save my life!'" (*Psalm 116:4* RSV).

2) "So do not be afraid of people. Do not be afraid of those who kill the body but cannot kill the soul ... even the hairs of your head have all been counted. So do not be afraid" (*Matthew 10:26-31*).

3) The proverb is affirmed in the story about the rich fool: "I do not have a place to keep all my crops—what can I do? Take life easy, eat, drink, and enjoy yourself!" But God said to him, "You fool! This very night you will have to give up your life" *(Luke 12:17-20).*

156. Umoza ndi nthazi

Oneness is strength

Expl: In an abundance of counselors, there is victory.

Meaning: Unity is strength.

Occasion: Applied to teach the value of cooperation and inter-dependence in the community. Preachers use it to exhort their fellow Christians to work together so that the Church may grow. Ministers advise newly married couples to live in unity because they are one body.

Related Biblical Themes and Stories:

1) "And though a man might prevail against one who is alone, two will withstand him. A threefold cord is not quickly broken" *(Ecclesiastes 4:12 RSV).*

2) "A man will leave his father and mother and unite with his wife, and the two will become one. So they are no longer two, but one" *(Mark 10:7).*

157. Ungabizgangapo chikumbu cha, njowi yijengi penipo

Do not dip your fingers, otherwise your nail will stick there

Expl: A person should examine his/her position carefully before involving himself/herself in incidents that may bring trouble.

Meaning: A person should not provoke situations because he/she happens to be in a group or knows about an incident.

Occasion: Cited to caution people against the dangers of mob action. Sometimes it is used to warn against provoking someone you really don't know well. Preachers use it to warn people against provoking God to anger.

Related Biblical Themes and Stories:

1) "They provoked the Lord to anger with their doings, and a plague broke out among them" *(Psalm 106:29 RSV).*

2) "They angered him at the waters of Meribah and it went ill with Moses on their account; for they made his spirit bitter, and he spoke words that were rash" *(Psalm 106:32* RSV*).*

158. Ungawona chipeli kuti chapo pa chanya, pasi pe moto

Do not look only at the cool surface of the porridge below there is heat.

Expl: The surface of porridge may look as if there is no heat under it. Yet if you dip your finger, you would burn yourself. The English equivalent is, "Appearances are deceptive."

Meaning: A person should be careful in his/her dealings with another, since the other person's outward show of friendship may be different from thoughts or intentions.

Occasion: Cited when cautioning a person about his/her dealings with someone he/she does not know well.

Related Biblical Themes and Stories:

1) "A hypocrite hides his hate behind flattering words" *(Proverbs 26:24).*

2) "Be on you guard against false prophets; they come to you looking like sheep on the outside, but on the inside they are really like wild wolves" *(Matthew 7:15)*

159. Uryiyengi wima

You will eat while standing

Expl: A person is restless because of something bad that he/she has done.

Meaning: You will not have peace.

Occasion: Cited when warning a person against putting much trust in someone who might leave one in trouble. Sometimes it is used to advise one against disregarding a person who helps one, or against doing a bad thing to a person who is supposed to help one.

Related Biblical Themes and Stories:

1) When Cain killed his brother Abel, he became a fugitive and wanderer in a foreign land *(Genesis 4:12-14).*

2) "Remember what I say, my son, and never forget what I tell you to do" *(Proverbs 7:1).*

160. Uyu ndi Chimbwi

This one is a hyena

Expl: The proverb is used symbolically to show a person who has knowledge of death and also courage to handle the corpse. The hyena is able to smell a dead animal from a long distance. Other people believe that a hyena dreams about where its prey can be found. *Mzukuru* is a similar term meaning a person who washes and dresses a corpse or those who carry out the burial of the dead person.

Meaning: A person who has some special knowledge of certain things—in this sense, one who first approaches the dead body.

Occasion: Cited when giving a title to people in the community who have some special role to play at a funeral.

Related Biblical Themes and Stories:

1) Joseph of Arimathea went to Pilate and asked for the body of Jesus. Then he took it down and wrapped it in a linen shroud, and laid him in a rock-hewn tomb where no one had ever yet been laid (*Luke 23:50-53*).

2) Nicodemus, who at first had gone to see Jesus at night, went with Joseph, taking with him about one hundred pounds of spices, a mixture of myrrh and aloes. The two men took Jesus' body and wrapped it in linen cloths with the spices according to the Jewish custom of preparing a body for burial (*John 19:39-40*).

161. Vimiti vyo vyepamoza vileka cha kuchita ng'wema

Trees that are together brush against each other

Expl: The analogy is taken from Tonga ecology. As one walks through the forest one hears the trees making noise as they brush against each other.

Meaning: It is obvious that people living together will quarrel sometimes. This needs to be accepted.

Occasion: Used to advise people who have quarreled to reconcile and continue to live together. The proverb has a court setting or is cited at a council of elders where various cases are brought to be judged. Young people are advised to forgive each other if they have disagreed on certain issues.

Related Biblical Themes and Stories:

The proverb can be related to the story of Martha from Luke 10:38-41. Martha is full of good works and entirely free from the selfishness that seeks its own pleasure—a fault which she thinks she detects in Mary. In a way this causes friction: Martha was upset over all the work she had to do, so she came and said, "Lord don't you care that my sister has left me to do all the work by myself? Tell her to come and help me" (*Luke 10:40*). But Martha earns a gentle reproof from Jesus because she has not yet learned that unselfishness, service, and even sacrifice can be spoiled by self-concern and self-pity. Good works which are not self-forgetful can become a misery to the doer and a tyranny to others (v. 41).

162. Vitotoka vigona mu chikuto chimoza cha

Two cockerels cannot sleep in one cage

Expl: People living in the same house or community cannot avoid friction.

Meaning: A village or community cannot be ruled by more than one leader.

Occasion: This proverb is used to disapprove one's unjustified challenge of the leader's authority in the same community. Sometimes when there is strife in a family, the wife is advised to submit herself to the husband.

Related Biblical Themes and Stories:

1) Any country that divides itself into groups which fight each other will not last very long. And any town or family that divides itself into groups which fight each other will fall apart (*Matthew 12:25*).

2) "When a strong man, with all his weapons ready, guards his own house, all his belongings are safe. But when a stronger man attacks him and defeats him, he carries away all the weapons the owner was depending on and divides up what he stole" (*Luke 11:21-22*).

163. Vuchi ndi malipilo

Your sweat is your wages

Expl: If you work hard, you can have plenty to support yourself and your family.

Meaning: A person should take initiative in order to earn a living.

Occasion: Used to advise someone to work hard so that one would not lack anything to eat. In other words, one should accept the fact that nothing good can come without working for it.

Related Biblical Themes and Stories:

1) "You will have to work hard and sweat to make the soil produce anything' *(Genesis 3:19)*.

2) "Whoever refuses to work is not allowed to eat" *(II Thessalonians 3:10)*.

164. Vya mzinga

She is surrounded (or tied up)

Expl: The analogy depicts a person who is surrounded by danger. *Maskawi* (spirit-possession) is common among Tonga women. Once the victim is attacked, she appears as if she is bound up, especially when having convulsions.

Meaning: She/he is spirit-possessed.

Occasion: Cited when sympathising with a person who is spirit-possessed. Some preachers refer this concept to the spirit-possessed people in the Bible.

Related Biblical Themes and Stories:

1) The Lord Jesus said that the evil spirit goes out and brings seven other spirits even worse than itself, and they come and live there. So when it is all over, that person is in worse shape than he was at the beginning (*Luke 11:24-26*).

2) "He was some distance away when he saw Jesus so he ran, fell on his knees before him, and screamed in a loud voice, 'Jesus, Son of the Most High God! What do you want with me? For God's sake, I beg you don't punish me'" (*Mark 5:6-8*).

3) "The next day an evil spirit from God suddenly took control of Saul and he raved in his house like a madman" (*I Samuel 18:10*).

165. Vyotikamba vya mng'ombe

We speak to the cattle

Expl: Cattle are not easily controlled. A cow will not retreat on crossing a road, even if one sounds a hooter. Cattle will give a deaf ear.

Meaning: There are people who turn a deaf ear when others are advising them.

Occasion: Used to advise young people to be obedient to what the elders of the community say, especially on changing their moral attitudes.

Related Biblical Themes and Stories:

The proverb addresses the theme of obedience:

1) In the Temple vision, Isaiah saw that the people of Judah were quite deaf in the way they constantly committed sin. So Isaiah brought the following message to the people: "No matter how much you listen, you will not understand. No matter how much you look, you will not know what is happening." Isaiah is to make the minds of the people dull, their ears deaf, and their eyes blind so that they cannot see or hear or understand. In other words, the people of Judah were so deaf that they could not even change their ways (*Isaiah 6:9-10*).

2) In the parable of the sower, those who pay deaf ear to the word of God are like seeds which fell on the path, rock and on thorn bushes (*Luke 8:11-14*).

166. Wabaya chiwanda

You have killed a spirit

Expl: It is the Tonga belief that certain creatures reincarnate the spirit or are spirit-form, e.g., a snake. Thus killing such a snake, (e.g., *Mlinga*, a short, stubby, blackish non-poisonious snake) is believed to be killing the spirit of someone.

Meaning: Cutting off the spirit's chance of visiting former haunts by killing the form it made use of.

Occasion: Used when warning people against killing certain creatures which are believed to be spirit-form. Usually, young people are advised not to kill any creature that comes around during a funeral ceremony.

Related Biblical Themes and Stories:

1) There was a large herd of pigs nearby, feeding on the hillside. So the spirits begged Jesus, "Send us to the pigs and let us go into them" (*Mark 5:11-13*).

2) "Is it lawful on the Sabbath to do good or to do harm, to save life or to kill?" (*Mark 3:4*).

167. Wabila pa chandi nutu uwoneka

You are drowned in a gourd, the head is seen

Expl: A gourd is a traditional drinking vessel. It can contain a small quantity of water to quench one's thirst. A big object cannot hide itself in such a small amount of water.

Meaning: We should not cover our sufferings because they reveal our weakness.

Occasion: Cited to warn people not to cover problems, because one day they will come to light. Often the advice is given to a young woman who hides her pregnancy, forgetting that one day everyone will see it. Thus, sufferings reveal our character. On the other hand, we advise young people to accept suffering as a challenge to life.

Related Biblical Themes and Stories:

1) Paul says, "More than that, we rejoice in our sufferings, knowing that suffering produces endurance, and endurance produces character and character produces hope, and hope does not disappoint us" (*Romans 5:3-4*).

2) "What ever you have said in the dark will be heard in broad daylight" (*Luke 12:3*).

168. Wafwiya limu

Dies once and for all

Expl: The saying points to the Tonga concept of a person's soul or life (*Mzimu, Umoyo*). As long as he/she breathes (*watuta,*) he/she is alive. When he/she dies once and for all, the departed spirit is called *Mzimu*. It is sometimes used metaphorically to refer to a person who is taken up completely by pleasures.

Meaning: The person is completely dead, but even then she/he still exists. His/her spirit still lives on in another state.

Occasion: Cited when a death has occurred, and *Mzukuru* (the person who first approaches the dead) has declared that the person is dead. Sometimes the proverb is used to warn those who are absent-minded or taken up by pleasures of the world, to change their attitudes.

Related Biblical Themes and Stories:

1) "Everyone has forgotten me, as though I were dead" *(Psalms 31:12).*

2) "Pilate was surprised to hear that Jesus was already dead. He called the army officer and asked him if Jesus had been dead a long time" *(Mark 15:44).*

3) "But a widow who gives herself to pleasure has already died, even though she lives" *(I Timothy 5:6).*

169. Wajinangiye weneko

Let them spoil it themselves

Expl: The proverb originated from a tale that a kind alligator used to salt beans for the girls in their absence to make the dish appetizing. However, the girls later on told their parents, who planned to kill it. When the alligator escaped, it said, "Let them spoil it themselves." Thus, people should not take hasty and unconsidered decisions.

Meaning: You should think carefully before taking an action.

Occasion: Used by preachers to warn people against rejecting Jesus who came to save us. It is also cited to advise people not to reject other people's good ideas, which may help them in the future.

Related Biblical Themes and Stories:

1) "The stone which the builders rejected as worthless turned out to be the most important of all" *(Mark 12:10).*

2) "People will look at him who they pierced" *(John 19:37).*

170. Wakozga kwa wiske

He is like his father

Expl: A child who behaves exactly in the manner the father does.

Meaning: People inherit their parents' characteristics.

Occasion: Cited when discussing a person's peculiar behaviour or unique talents that might reflect parents or direct relatives, e.g., hard work, wisdom, courage, and so on.

Related Biblical Themes and Stories:

1) "He always had the nature of God, but he did not think that by force he should try to become equal with God" (*Philippians 2:6*).

2) "Christ is the visible likeness of the invisible God. He is the first-born Son, superior to all created things" (*Colossians 1:1*).

3) "Whoever has seen me has seen the Father" (*John 14:9*).

4) "So that they may be one just as you and I are one" *(John 17:21).*

171. Wakuya ku muzi ukuru

He/she has gone to a great city

Expl: Death in Tonga society is a journey to a great home where one is received by one's ancestors.

Meaning: He/she has joined the majority who have died.

Occasion: Used when someone is dead. The people often speak of the dead as joining the ancestors. It is advice that where the dead people go is an even safer place than we have in this life. Preachers often use it as a way of consolation to the bereaved.

Related Biblical Themes and Stories:

1) Jesus said, "There are many rooms in my Father's house, and I am going to prepare a place for you. I would not tell you this if it were not so. And after I go and prepare a place for you I will come back and take you to myself; so that you will be where I am" (*John 14:2-3*).

2) "And I saw the Holy City, the New Jerusalem coming down out of heaven from God" (*Revelation 21:2-4*).

3) "For Abraham was waiting for the city which God has designed and built, the city with permanent foundations" (*Hebrews 11:10*).

4) "I will some day go to where he is, but he can never come back to me" (*2 Samuel 12:23*).

172. Waliya vuwa, waliya ulambwi

If you cry for rain, you also cry for mud

Expl: Sometimes the good things we need for our lives also can spoil our lives. For example, we need rains, but flood can cause loss of life. When rainwater soaks the soil, it leaves much mud on the ground, making it difficult to pass through or work on.

Meaning: If you desire a good thing, you should also be prepared for any difficulties that may follow.

Occasion: Cited when people begin to complain about a prolonged rainy season, which may bring about disaster on the lives of the people.

Related Biblical Themes and Stories:

1) When the people of Israel asked for a king, Samuel was displeased because the king would ill-treat them, among other evils. Some of their sons would be slaves to plow the fields *(I Samuel 8:4-17).*

2) When the wife of Zebedee asked Jesus to give her two sons places of honor in his kingdom, Jesus asked them, "Can you drink the cup of suffering that I am about to drink?" *(Matthew 20:20-28).*

173. Wamuchontha muguto

To prick a person in the ear

Expl: To make someone understand or to convince a person.

Meaning: To give a person enough evidence.

Occasion: Usually cited in court before a judge or a jury or at a council for the elders (*Mphara*), when one is defending himself/herself in order to convince the jury.

Related Biblical Themes and Stories:

1 "Tell me where did John's authority to baptise come from, was it from God or from man?" *(Mark 11:29-31).*

174. Wanthu mbanthu wakuwaziwa ndi Mnkhwere

Human beings are known by a baboon

Expl: A baboon is shrewd enough to spy on people and see what a person tries to do in secret. For example, if a person wants to trap a baboon, it will see from up the tree where the person has set the trap.

Meaning: We should not think that no one knows the things that we have done in secret.

Occasion: Cited when advising a person to be honest, because everything done in secret will one day be disclosed.

Related Biblical Themes and Stories:

1) The Bible teaches that God has complete knowledge of us, so we cannot hide anything from Him. Darkness and light is the same to God *(Psalm 139:7-12)*.

2) "Whatever is now covered up will be uncovered, and every secret will be made known" *(Matthew 10:26)*.

3) "The dead were judged according to what they had done, as recorded in the books" *(Revelation 20:12)*.

175. Watipitiya

To look fresh

Expl: The picture is that of a fresh shoot sprouting up with healthy new branches. It is metaphorically used to refer to someone who is steadily growing up in body and mind.

Meaning: A person who looks healthy and young.

Occasion: Cited in praise of a person who looks after his/her health properly. The body looks fresh and smooth, even though he/she is advanced in age.

Related Biblical Themes and Stories:

1) "The royal line of David is like a tree that has been cut down; but just as new branches sprout from a stump, so a new King will arise from among David's descendants" *(Isaiah 11:1)*.

2) "Jesus grew both in body and in wisdom, gaining favour with God and men" *(Luke 2:52)*.

176. Wavimyantha

You have tasted it

Expl: One who is punished for the wrong thing one has done.

Meaning: To receive punishment for the evil that a person has done.

Occasion: Used to mock one who is punished for the wrong thing he/she has done. It is also used in a court verdict to taunt a convicted person.

Related Biblical Themes and Stories:

1) The proverb is affirmed in the words of the penitent criminal on the cross, who said to the other: "Do you not fear God? You received the same sentence he did. Ours, however, is only right, because we are getting what we deserve for what we did; but he has done no wrong" *(Luke 23:40-41).*

2) "Do not deceive yourselves; no one makes a fool of God. A person will reap exactly what he sows" *(Galatians 6:7).*

177. Wavituta

Belonging to the spirits

Expl: This refers to a person who is drawn by the spirits. Usually this manifests itself in an alteration of the consciousness, personality, or will of the individual.

Meaning: A form of trance in which the behaviour or actions of a person are interpreted as evidence of a control by a spirit normally external to his/her.

Occasion: Cited often when the spirit-possessed begins to make the hee-heeing and muttering sounds. This is very common among the bereaved at the mourning of their beloved ones. Preachers also use it to refer to demon-possessed people who were healed by Jesus. Spirit-possessed people detect witches around their homes.

Related Biblical Themes and Stories:

1) When the seven sons of Sceva were spirit-possessed they said, "I know Jesus, and I know about Paul but you—who are you?" *(Acts 19:14-15).*

2) In the Synagogue was a man who had the spirit of an evil demon in him; he screamed out in a loud voice, "Ah! what do you want with us, Jesus of Nazareth? Are you here to destroy us? I know who you are: You are

God's holy messenger!" Jesus ordered the spirit, "Be quiet and come out of the man!" (*Luke 4: 33-35*).

3) In the story about the healing of a boy with an evil spirit, as soon as the spirit saw Jesus, it threw the boy into a fit, so that he fell on the ground and rolled around, foaming at the mouth (*Mark 9:20-22*).

178. Wawi mbanthu kekija nkha nyama

Two are people, one is an animal

Expl: A person should not take chances to travel alone at night or in places of danger.

Meaning: A person who travels with a friend is more secure than a person who travels alone.

Occasion: Used to warn people against taking a chance travelling alone at night. Sometimes it is used as an encouragement to young people who would like to marry.

Related Biblical Themes and Stories:

1) "Two men can resist an attack that would defeat one man alone" *(Ecclesiastes 4:12)*.

2) "Do not be afraid—I will save you. When you pass through deep waters, I will be with you" *(Isaiah 43:1-2)*.

179. Wawona masu gha chulu ghatema

You should not always expect flying ants to fly just because you saw their holes opening on a heap

Expl: Usually flying ants fly out during the early rainy season. Some of these are edible. But they are unpredictable even if they sometimes show signs of flying. Yet people become impatient if they do not fly out.

Meaning: A person should wait patiently, for everything has its own time.

Occasion: Cited to warn those people who are so anxious over things that they become impatient and frustrated. There is need to become patient and wait for the right time. Also, young people should not rely too much on promises from others because they might not materialise. So it is important to be patient and self-reliant.

Related Biblical Themes and Stories:

The proverb addresses the theme of self-reliance and patience:

1) Everything that happens in this world happens at the time God chooses (*Ecclesiastes 3:1*). We live in a world of changes. In the wheel of nature, sometimes one spoke is uppermost and by and by the contrary; there is a constant ebbing and flowing, waxing and waning from one extreme to the other.

2) On anxiety, Jesus' advice is, "So do not start worrying where will my food come from? or my drink? or my clothes? Your Father in heaven knows that you need all these things" (*Matthew 6:31-34*). More than almost anything else, our Lord Jesus largely and earnestly warns his disciples against the sin of those disquieting, distracting, distrustful cares of this life.

180. Wazamukumana ndi aweya wa mujino, mumphunu ulimu kale

You will meet people with hairy teeth, while they already have hair in their nostrils

Expl: There are fiercer people than we have ever met.

Meaning: People should not disobey or disregard their elders or parents.

Occasion: Cited when warning unruly young people against despising others, because some day they will meet extraordinary people who will be over them. It is a strong warning to those who feel that their malicious acts are not known by others. Sometimes the proverb is used to advise those who take things for granted and do not take care of their lives.

Related Biblical Themes and Stories:

1) Eli always advised his sons to behave. But the sons always did what displeased God. The warnings that Eli gave did not mean anything to the children: "Stop it, my sons! This is an awful thing the people of the Lord are talking about. If a man sins against another man, God can defend him, but who can defend a man who sins against the Lord?" (*I Samuel 2:24-25*).

2) Some boys made fun of Elisha, "Get out of here, baldy!" Elisha turned around and cursed them in the name of the Lord. Then two she-bears

came out of the woods and tore forty-two of the boys into pieces (*2 Kings 2:23-24*). This is what the proverbs would imply.

181. Wendi jisu la Nkhwazi

He/she has a fish eagle's eye

Expl: A fish eagle can see its prey from a long distance. The proverb is used as a simile.

Meaning: She/he has a sharp eye which is like an eagle's eye.

Occasion: Cited when a person recognizes others from a long distance, especially in a crowd. Sometimes it is used to praise one who finds a lost thing that required a long search.

Related Biblical Themes and Stories:

1) "She lights a lamp, sweeps her house, and looks carefully everywhere until she finds it" (*Luke 15:8*).

2) "He was still a long way from home when his father saw him, his heart was filled with pity, and he ran, threw his arms around his son and kissed him" (*Luke 15:20*).

182. Wendi kamlomo kakuthwa

He/she has a sharp mouth

Expl: It reflects a person who is clever in handling a case, or in the way one helps in the settlement of cases brought before a council of elders.

Meaning: A person who is supreme judge in a court case.

Occasion: Used when a person helping in the adjudication of a case concludes his/her contribution and invites the court to listen to the final person.

Related Biblical Themes and Stories:

1) The proverb can be used to show how Gamaliel handled the Apostles' case: "Leave them alone! If what they have planned and done is of human origin it will disappear, but if it comes from God, you cannot possibly defeat them. You could find yourselves fighting against God!" The Council followed Gamaliel's advice (*Acts 5: 33-39*).

183. Wendi mzimu uheni

He has a bad spirit

Expl: The spirit which works evil against or torments a person.

Meaning: A restless spirit which is always bloodthirsty.

Occasion: Cited when warning a person against associating with bad or` murderous people. Sometimes it is spoken to refer to a person who is possessed with an evil spirit, such as a madman. Sometimes it is used to refer to a proud person. Some preachers use it to condemn those with bad behaviour.

Related Biblical Themes and Stories:

1) "The Lord's spirit left Saul, and an evil spirit sent by the Lord tormented him" (*I Samuel 16:14*).

2) "Pride goes before destruction and haughty spirit before a fall" (*Proverbs 16:18*).

3) "Then Herod, when he saw that he had been tricked by the wise men, was in a furious rage and he sent and killed all the male children in Bethlehem and in all that region who were two years old or under" (*Matthew 2:16*).

184. Wendi mzimu wamampha

He/she has a good spirit

Expl: It is the sense in which the Tonga speak of a living man having a guardian spirit.

Meaning: A person who has a good guardian spirit who looks after him/her.

Occasion: Refers to those people who have a healthy life. In most cases it is used to refer to a person who has good luck i.e., the spirit of one's ancestors guards the person in the right way or when the spirit of one's ancestor does not work against one. Preachers also use it to refer to role models of good Christian spirit in the community.

Related Biblical Themes and Stories:

1) God is to take some of the good spirit in Moses and give it to the people in order to assist Moses in some tasks (*Numbers 11:17*).

2) "It is the spirit of Almighty God that comes to men and gives them wisdom" (*Job. 32:8*).

3) "But my servant Caleb, because he has a different spirit and has followed me fully, I will bring into the land into which he went, and his descendants shall possess it" (*Numbers 14:24*).

185. Yo pamuko pa moyo ndiyo wajura kukhomo

He/she who has a stomach-ache is the one who struggles with the door

Expl: The proverb is derived from a legend about conditions in the past days, when, due to the roaming about of wild animals, it was expected that anyone who would go outside at night to ease himself/herself would be escorted. Still, he/she would take a risk opening the door, and someone awakened by the noise would courteously go out with him/her.

Meaning: A person in need or in difficulty should take the initiative towards remedying the situation, in order to encourage others to come to his aid.

Occasion: Used when encouraging a person to take initiative in doing something before he/she asks someone to assist him/her. A person should not wait for external assistance before putting one's effort into it first. Sometimes it is used in a court setting. The one concerned should take the case to the court. Young people should develop the spirit of initiative.

Related Biblical Themes and Stories:

1) Jesus said, "People who are well do not need a doctor, but only those who are sick" (*Mark 2:17*).

2) The Lord says, "Come everyone who is thirsty, here is water! Come, you that have no money—buy grain and eat! Come! Buy wine and milk—it will cost you nothing" (*Isaiah 55:1*).

3) "Come to me all of you who are tired from carrying heavy loads, and I will give you rest" (*Matthew 11:28*).

186. Yo waswela mviheni wariyengi

A person who delays correcting things will end up crying

Expl: This has a similar meaning to the English proverb, "A stitch in time saves nine."

Meaning: A solution taken in good time saves one from a big problem later on.

Occasion: Sometimes used in preaching, admonishing those who do not make up their minds to repent from sinning. These people find themselves taken up by the events, and later lament. In other instances, the proverb is used to advise a person whose property needs to be attended to before it gets worse. Young people are advised to prepare for their future from early stages of their lives.

Related Biblical Themes and Stories:

The theme of decision making comes clearly in this proverb:

1) Jesus warned some people to turn away from their sins, "No indeed. And I tell you that if you do not turn from your sins, you will all die" (*Luke 13:3,5*).

2) Again in the theme of judgment, the ten virgins of Matthew 25:1-13 illustrate this proverb clearly. One must prepare and make a decision before it is too late. The five foolish virgins found the door closed.

187. Yo watemda ndi mnkhungu nayo wawengi mnkhungu

One who walks with a thief will also become a thief

Expl: If one person in a group is bad, then his/her behaviour will affect others.

Meaning: Often our behaviour is affected by joining wrong peer groups.

Occasion: Used to advise young people not to join peer groups who are habitual drunkards, drug abusers, smokers, and so on; because it is easy to imitate what they do, only to find in the end that their life is ruined.

Related Biblical Themes and Stories:
The proverb reflects advice Paul gives to the Thessalonians:

1) "It may be that someone there will not obey the message we send you in this letter. If so, take note of him and have nothing to do with him so that he will be ashamed" (*2 Thessalonians 3:14*).

2) "Don't associate with people who drink too much wine or stuff them-selves with food. Drunkards and gluttons will be reduced to poverty. If all you do is eat and sleep, you will soon be wearing rags" (*Proverbs 23:20-21*).

3) Come and join us, and we'll all share what we steal. Son, don't go with people like that. Stay away from them (*Proverbs 1:10-15*).

4) "Don't be envious of evil people, and don't try to make friends with them. Causing trouble is all they ever think about. Every time they open their mouth, someone is going to be hurt" (*Proverbs 24:1-2*).

5) "Keep company with the wise and you will become wise. If you make friends with stupid people you will be ruined" (*Proverbs 13:20*).

188. Yo watondo wasunga, yo wataya waliya

The one who finds keeps, the one who loses weeps

Expl: People should keep account of what they find.

Meaning: A person should be responsible, and not become extravagant.

Occasion: Used to ridicule people who do not keep their jobs or what they have, thinking that they can always have new chances. By time their hopes fail to materialise, newly acquired things or relationships will prove useless, and, they lose everything.

Related Biblical Themes and Stories:

1) "So each of us shall give account of himself to God" (*Romans 14:12*).

2) "Now, take the money away from him and give it to the one who has ten thousand coins. For to every person who has something, even more will be given, and he will have more than enough; but the person who has nothing, even the little that he has will be taken away from him. As for this useless servant—throw him outside in the darkness; there he will cry and gnash his teeth" (*Matthew 25:28-30*).

189. Yo watuwapo pano ndiyo waruta, kweni kuti nkhamusi-yeso ku masanu, ndakana

The one who has left me should go! But as for me to leave one in the grave, I can't

Expl: It is a lamentation to express the sad fact that one who dies goes for good. It is an acceptance of the shock that comes to a person when his/her beloved one is dead.

Meaning: We expect in future to meet those who have died.

Occasion: Cited to express grief when a beloved one has died. It also implies hope to those living, that one day they too shall follow the living dead.

Related Biblical Themes and Stories:

1) The proverb can be affirmed in the words of David at the death of his child: "But now he is dead; why should I fast? Can I bring him back again? I shall go to him, but he will not return to me" *(II Samuel 12:23).*

2) The Bible teaches that at the resurrection, the living and the dead will meet and be with the Lord *(I Thessalonians 4:13-17).*

190. Yo waziwa vyose ndi Chiuta

The one who knows everything is God

Expl: The Tonga believe that God is the Supreme Spirit, the self-existent one who knows everything. He is not a departed spirit.

Meaning: God knows everything, even things done in secret.

Occasion: Cited in making self-defense in a court setting. The accuser may be alleged to have done something wrong but he/she would cite the proverb as a way of defense or swearing. It implies a challenge to God to pursue or punish him/her if he/she is in the wrong.

Related Biblical Themes and Stories:

1) "Your knowledge of me is too deep, it is beyond my understanding" *(Psalm 139:6).*

2) "But when you help a needy person, do it in such a way that even your closest friend will not know about it. Then it will be a private matter. And your Father, who sees what you do in private, will reward you" *(Matthew 6:4).*

3) "Jesus answered, 'I have always spoken publicly to everyone; all my teaching was done in the Synagogue and in the Temple, where all the people come together. I have never said anything in secret. Why, then, do you question me? Ask them what I told them—they know what I said'" *(John 18:20-21).*

191. Zeru zakuwija zibayiska

Self-conceit can kill a person

Expl: Individualism and self-conceit is discouraged in the Tonga community.

Meaning: It is better to mix with others in order to learn from their ideas and ways of life. In other words, we need to live in harmony with others.

Occasion: Used when advising a young person who isolates himself/herself from others or when warning a selfish person. When problems overtake you, others will not come to assist you.

Related Biblical Themes and Stories:

1) In the "priestly prayer" of John 17, Jesus prays for the disciples, "that they may be one" *(John 17:11).*

2) Here too the idea of "Unity is strength" comes very clearly. The picture we see in the early Church is that of people living in harmony and sharing things in common. Those who believed "were together and had all things in common; and they sold their possessions and goods and distributed them to all as any had need" *(Acts 2:44-47).*

192. Ziulikanga zikumpoka mahomwa

The one who was late was overtaken by a battle

Expl: In a battle one needs to make quick decisions.

Meaning: Those who are late will find themselves overtaken by events or may miss blessings.

Occasion: Cited when people do not heed advice, especially when young people are not fully prepared to withstand certain circumstances with readiness and awareness.

Related Biblical Themes and Stories:

1) In the parable of the ten virgins our Lord Jesus warns us not to be late in making a decision to enter the Kingdom of God, i.e., accepting His Word. It will be too late when we shall realize that we are in trouble. We are therefore to keep watching *(Matthew 25:1-13).*

2) Likewise, in Mark 13:32-37, Jesus warns us to be ready all the time, for we do not know when that day or hour will come, neither angels in

heaven nor the son, only the Father knows. We have to watch because we do not know when the master of the house is coming. If he comes suddenly, he must not find us asleep.

3) Isaac began to tremble and shake all over and he asked, "Who was it, then, who killed an animal and brought it to me? I ate it just before you came, I gave him my final blessing, and so it is his forever" (*Genesis 27:20-35*).

193. Zua limoza kuti liwozga nyama ya Njovu cha

One day cannot make an elephant rot

Expl: An elephant is the biggest animal and it cannot rot within a day. If we come back tomorrow, we will still be able to take some meat from it. Therefore we should not fear when we have to postpone other jobs in order to attend to more urgent ones.

Meaning: It is not harmful to postpone one's work to the next day.

Occasion: Cited when persuading a person to put off what he/she is doing for some time in order to facilitate his/her involvement in some other pressing issues. For instance, students should learn to prioritise their study schedules.

Related Biblical Themes and Stories:

1) God is going to judge the righteous and the evil alike because every-thing, every work will happen at its own time (*Ecclesiastes 3:17*).

2) Jesus said, "What if one of you has a sheep and it falls into a deep hole on the Sabbath. Will he not take hold of it and lift it out?" (*Matthew 12:11*).

3) "As long as it is day I must do the work of him who sent me, night is coming when no one can work" (*John 9:4*).

194. Zunguliyane, ine ndizunguliyengi uku tikumanenge kurweka

If you go round the one side, I'll go round the other and so we will meet at the back

Expl: This is a hope that although people die at different times, one day they will meet again.

Meaning: Death is not the end of everything.

Occasion: Used to give hope to people that death is not the end of life, because they shall meet their beloved ones one day. Thus, the proverb is cited during funerals. It is also cited when one is prepared to suffer for others.

Related and Stories:

1) "Then Jesus went with his disciples to a place called Gethsemane and he said to them, 'Sit here while I go over there and pray'" (*Matthew 26:26*).

2) "The sorrow in my heart is so great that it almost crushes me. Stay here and keep watch with me" (*Matthew 26:38*).

Bibliography

Banda, Joseph T.K., "Proverbs in Tonga: Proverbs N.M. 35740," unpublished, 1985.

Chirwa, Filemon K., *Nthanu za Chitonga*, Livingstonia Mission, 1932.

MacAlpine, A.G., "Tonga Beliefs and Customs," *Aurora* 8, Livingstonia Mission, 1905.

Schoffeleers Matthews, and A.A. Roscoe. *Land of Fire: Oral Literature from Malawi*, Blantyre: Montfort Press, 1985.

Velsen, Jan van, *The Politics of Kinship: A Study in Social Manipulation among the Lakeside Tonga of Nyasaland.* Manchester University Press, 1964.

Mphande David K., "On the Use of Tonga Myths, Folktales and Proverbs in Moral Education", PhD University of Malawi, 2001.

Mphande David K., *Nthanthi za Chitonga za Kuzambizgiya ndi Kutauliya*, Kachere: Zomba, 2000.

Nyambe, Sumbwa, *Zambian Proverbs*, Lusaka Multimedia Publication, 1993.

Soko B.J., "Tonga Proverbs," Unpublished Collection, 1995.

Index: By Scripture Reference

This index includes only the 195 proverbs annotated in Part II above, not the supplementary list of 116 proverbs in Appendix A

.

Appendix A: 116 Further Tonga Proverbs for Study and Application

1 Afwiti mbanasi

Wizards are relatives

Expl: A person who can hurt you may be the one who is close to you.

2 Akufwa apaska nchitu

Dead people give us a job

Expl: When someone dies everyone is concerned about plans for conducting burial activities, feeding people who come to attend the funeral, etc.

3 Amtekwa

Disabled

Expl: More or less like a metaphor, meaning a person who stops from place to place.

4 Amunkhwele asekana viphata

Baboons laugh at each other's bare pads

Expl: We should not despise one another.

5 Amwenda-natu

A double dealer

Expl: A person who is a liar.

6 Anyamata azomphe

To let young people take the message quickly

Expl: To run with a message before it is too late.

7 Asani kunthazi nkhwamampha, kuvuli nkhwamampha yikamba ndi nyezi

It is a fly that indicates whether your journey and destiny is good

Expl: There are signs to indicate failure or success in life.

8 Azamsaniya nchalanga chitenje bu!

They will find that you are dead!

Expl: A person should be careful in order to keep away from danger.

9 Chakuziwanizga chingulinda chirwane

That which was late was waiting for danger

Expl: It is not good to wait too long lest you be overtaken by other things or danger.

10 Chanju che mu manja

Love is in the shaking of hands

Expl: Shaking hands is a sign of love/affection.

11 Chawa mu maso ghaki

It is fallen in his/her eyes

Expl: A person who has seen a thing/or one bearing responsibility.

12 Chimeza mankhwawa

A glutton

Expl: A person who is greedy.

13 Chiruwa chakuruwa mbavi pa phewa

Forgetfulness is like one forgetting an ax on his shoulder

Expl: A person who forgets that a thing he/she looks for is in his/her hands or pockets, or on the shoulder.

14 Chiruwa chilivi munkhwara

Forgetfulness has no medicine

Expl: Every person can forget something at one time or another.

15 Cho chawona ine charutapo mawa che paku iwe

What has seen me is gone; tomorrow it will see you

Expl: We should not rejoice when other people are in trouble.

16 Cho chiwenge pano nchaku tose

That which will happen here is for us all

Expl: Some events affect people corporately/or affect the whole group or family.

17 Cho walutapo nchaku cha

What you have passed by is not yours

Expl: What one has missed is not his/hers.

18 Dele laku lenduka

Slippery like ochre

Expl: A person who is very lazy.

19 Dolora nkhali

A person who breaks a pot

Expl: A greedy person.

20 Epa napo abikanga mtama kwene le ukume mchira

In a neighbouring home they boiled maize and they grew a tail

Expl: A person who was sick has just recovered.

21 Fukunyuwane makutu ghachiri nja

To unveil the news so that the ears might

Expl: A person should explain what actually had happened to him/her.

22 Fumbanane mungabayana waka

Ask one another or reason together, lest you kill one another

Expl: People should reason together when a conflict arises.

23 Garu walondo kweniko atimupong'e viwanga

A dog loves to go where he receives the bones

Expl: A person likes to go to places where there can be safety for his/her life.

24 Gonani ndikubayeni we patali cha

Sleep and I-will-kill-you is not a difficult thing

Expl: When a person is asleep anyone can do harm to him/her.

25 Jisu likuntha nyoli cha, gho ghakuntha nyoli ndi manja

An eye does not take away a chicken's feathers, but the hands do

Expl: Our eyes look at anything that comes across.

26 Kakuziya maze

That which comes suddenly

Expl: There are things happening without being expected.

27 "Kamuzunguzeni" wangujiguziya nyifwa

"Kamuzunguzeni" brought death upon himself

Expl: A person should not imitate someone's habits without knowing their consequences.

28 Kanyele kangutuma Njovu

An ant sent an elephant

Expl: The young can ask an elderly person to assist in a problem.

29 Khungulukutu ngwe chimpara tukumu

At early dawn

Expl: Rising up very early in the morning.

30 Ko kabira boza kabuka

A log which is not heavy will always float

Expl: A person who pretends to be good might be caught one day as a hypocrite.

31 Ko yikuwa kayuzi

It is where it blows a whistle

Expl: A severe famine.

32 Kuchelera nkhuvwa tambala

To be early is to hear a cock-crow

Expl: If a person wants to be early, he/she should start at cock-crow.

33 Kugomore thusi mphamulenji-lenji

To make ridges is to be very early

Expl: A person can do better work or more work by beginning earlier. Equivalent is "An early bird catches the worm":

34 Kuja kauru ka unkhaka

To meet as a council of elders

Expl: When elders gather to decide on matters of deep concern, e.g. death.

35 Kuja nge mba Pusi mbwenu waka tafu-tafu

To sit like the chewing monkeys

Expl: A person who has nothing else to do.

36 Kujumpha chichinyiya chawapapi nkhujidaniya soka

To disobey parents' instructions is to invite death

Expl: A person should not overlook advice from parents.

37 Kukamba chiuvwa-uvwa

To speak senselessly

Expl: A person who is not logical in his/her speeches.

38 Kulauska munthurumi ndi chivivivi

To feed a husband is to give him early morning food

Expl: A wife should see that a husband is well cared for.

39 Kunyeta nge maji ghanyeta pa chipopomo

To be as slippery as water running down a waterfall

Expl: Something that is done quietly.

40 Kupambana kwa munkhwele ndi mbulika

A miss like that between a baboon and flying ants

Expl: A person who does not target the right time and misses something very important.

41 Kupangandiya minyu nkhuziwanizga kwa mpapi

For a child to get his/her teeth twisted is due to parents' carelessness

Expl: Certain habits worsen in people just because they are not checked from the early stages.

42 Kurya kwa mteki-teki

To eat everything at once

Expl: A person who is not economical enough, but rather extravagant.

43 Kurya Pusi ndi mutu waki

To eat a monkey's flesh and its head

Expl: To be foolish.

44 Kusele pambula kupupa

To escape through uncleared bush

Expl: To escape abruptly.

45 Kutiryiya masuku pa mutu

To eat fruits called "masuku" on people's heads

Expl: To cheat or bribe people.

46 Kutuzga kadonthu pa msana

To pick a dot on one's back

Expl: To clarify a point or to clear someone.

47 Kuvwiya mu kayuni

To hear from a bird

Expl: Not officially informed.

48 Kuwe ndi chirewa

To come back with a gift

Expl: To win a crown.

49 Kuwonana nge nkhu tulo

To see each other as in a dream

Expl: To meet once in a blue moon, or to meet rarely.

50 Kuyenda mchapu

To be in a hurry

Expl: To take a message fast, as when carrying a message about a death.

51 Kwadumuwanje tafipa mtima

What has passed across? We are frightened

Expl: Excitement or astonishment for seeing a strange face.

52 Kwenda chakudumuka mutu

To walk as if one's head is cut off

Expl: A person who is careless in his/her dealings or movements.

53 Kwende pa msana

To walk by the back

Expl: To be proud/satisfied with what he/she has.

54 Makani ghatenda ghija, munyinu watimugumuliyani magumu-gumu

The case walks as one defends one's self

Expl: A person who defends himself/herself well in a case.

55 Makutu ghachiri nja

The ears should be fed

Expl: An appeal to give a sound statement, as in a court case.

56 Masozi ghayoyokengi

Tears should drop

Expl: To be charitable.

57 Matenda ghakuchita kung'anamurizga

A person critically ill

Expl: A person who needs support.

58 Mbavi yifwiya mu lumono

An ax may be broken even by soft wood

Expl: A person should be careful and not take things for granted.

59 Mbewa yasoni yingufwiya kuzenji

A shy mouse died in a hole

Expl: A person should be courageous to defend herself/himself.

60 Mbiri yamampha yi jumbha chuma

Good reputation surpasses money

Expl: A good person is more respected than a bad person who may have acquired much wealth.

61 Mbunu njiheni yitaya mwakundawona

Greed is bad because it leads one into unseen trouble

Expl: A person who is greedy can end up in a big trouble.

62 Mbuzi yambura masengwe

A goat without horns

Expl: A person who cannot reason with others.

63 Mbuzi yisangaluka asane malonda ghepafupi

A goat becomes happy when it is about to be sold
Expl: A person begins to enjoy success when he/she is about to die.

64 Mlanga ndi mheni cha, kweni mheni ndi tiringanenge

An instructor is not a bad person, but one who says, "Let us be the same"
Expl: Care should be taken when a person chooses a company or peers.

65 Mlimu wamampha ndi wakusangaruska wendi marumbu ghamampha

A good and admirable work deserves commendable rewards
Expl: A person is praised for heroic things he/she has done.

66 Motu ukuwa ndi kuphutiriya

Fire grows as one blows it
Expl: A person should persevere for better results when doing some work.

67 Mpheti yangu cheza undipaske cho ndikhumba

My ring, "Give me what I want to have"
Expl: A person should not expect something which he/she has not worked for.

68 Mtiti wangujitukumuwa pa ulemu wo wanguronde

A sparrow misused someone's authority
Expl: We should respect those in authority.

69 Muchuwa wanguzizwa mu maji muchiwa mwaki

A frog was astonished while in its own water
Expl: There are things that happen without realizing that we caused them to happen.

70 Mumphika wakuchichizga usweka

If you force a pot it will break
Expl: You cannot force a horse to drink; or, we should not force something to happen.

71 Mutinge ndikamwanda, foja pe wazindiwa pa mtima

Tobacco alone can upset one's stomach without something else

Expl: We should not be hard-hearted toward others, especially in business dealings.

72 Muyuzi wagalu ngumoza

A dog has one shed

Expl: A person should be satisfied with what he/she has.

73 Mwa wakukunkhuzgika-kunkhuzgika kuti uchita ndeli cha

A rolling stone does not gather any moss

Expl: A person should not leave a job just because he/she thinks they will find another one.

74 Nchinkhu tyeku, ndi ng'o

Better to eat a little than never

Expl: It is better to have something than nothing. English equivalent is, "Half a loaf is better than no bread".

75 Ndachita nge ndalota

It is as if I dream

Expl: A chance that has come unexpectedly.

76 Ndafwiya kubala

I am dead because of bearing children

Expl: A person can suffer for the cause of others.

77 Ndalama zingubaya Yesu

Money killed Jesus

Expl: Too much love of money can affect our behaviour.

78 Ndali yenge vyamba

Politics is like Indian hemp (*chamba*)

Expl: In politics people behave as if they are confused.

79 Ndimba ya maji gha moto

A depth of very hot water

Expl: A person who is dangerous.

80 Nja yemu jino

Hunger is a tooth

Expl: A hungry person can be satisfied with little food.

81 Nthowa yimoza yibizga mu mathawali

One way leads to a dirty pool

Expl: A person should have alternatives in order to solve problems.

82 Nyaliwezga wawezga

Dusk sends us back home

Expl: A person realizes a mistake when it is too late.

83 Nyamakazi yabaya msana

Rheumatism kills the back

Expl: A person who is weak.

84 Odi! Odi! Odi! Potateke pano tiryepo

Listen to the announcement so that we can be fed

Expl: It is a formula often used during Tonga funerals to alert the people for an announcement.

85 Pa mphunu ndipa mlomo

Nose to mouth

Expl: A person who is overtaken by troubles.

86 Pa wanthu wo nawo nditenere kuti ndiwalereske

To look at important figures

Expl: To announce a message to some important people attending a function or funeral.

87 Saza lisazga bweka

Play can include everything

Expl: "Not all play makes Jack a good boy"; one must be careful the way one handles things.

88 Skapato yimoza avwala wanthu wawi cha

One shoe cannot be put on by two people

Expl: There are things you may not share, e.g., a wife.

89 Soni zingubaya Nkhwali

Pity killed Francolin

Expl: A person should not be shy to ask for a thing.

90 Thenga abaya cha

A messenger should never be killed

Expl: You do not kill an important person.

91 Tireke kudumbizga anyidu weniwo suzgu yawakwindika, chifukwa mawaliya ye paku iwe

Never rejoice about anyone's trouble because next time it will be yours

Expl: We should not rejoice when our friends are in trouble.

92 Tiziwa kuwa ndi marusu ghakuzizikiya anyake ndikweni ghazamukutizi-zika taweni pavuli

We can trick others but next time the same tricks will be played on us

Expl: We should not imitate the habits that we really do not know.

93 Uchembele nkhuryiyana

Kinship is to share food with others.

Expl: Do what you expect others to do for you.

94 Ulemu wamunyako muleke kukwamphuwa mutenele kukhorwa ndicho mwe nacho

Do not snatch someone's respect; be satisfied with what you have

Expl: Self-respect is important.

95 Ulowi ndi nyanga cha, ulowi mpha mlomo

Fear the mouth and not witchcraft

Expl: The tongue can be more destructive.

96 Unamana mburyayuni

Childishness is like a soft mushroom

Expl: The reasoning ability of a child is very low.

97 Unandi utaska

Many make a good defense

Expl: Unity is strength.

98 Vyaku Fu vyakuryiya lwandi

A tortoise's food is unsparingly eaten

Expl: We should learn to share with others. What you expect others to do for you, you should also do for them.

99 Vyambu sazi vyambura malaka

Fish called "*chambo*" (talapia) without scales arrayed on a string

Expl: A person who is confused for he/she cannot decide what to do.

100 Vyamunthazi viziwikwa cha

The future is not known

Expl: It is not easy to predict the future.

101 Wafwapu waka kasima nkhamunkhwala

Food mixed with medicine is not shared

Expl: One has no share.

102 Wajirengeska nge kathumba kapa Chiwaza, ko kaputiya pe

It is a shameful thing to be like a dirty bag blowing at an airport

Expl: A person should be careful with what he/she says in a group.

103 Waka aja nge mbakufwa

They are like dead people

Expl: There are people who are helpless as if they are dead.

104 Waku ngwaku, wamunyako watikusuzula

Your child is yours, the one who is not yours will go back to his/her parents

Expl: A child who is yours will always be dependable.

105 Wakusiliyane zila

To leave you with an egg

Expl: A person who is caring for somebody's child.

106 Wamakhate atimupusika skapato cha

You cannot cheat a leper out of a pair of shoes

Expl: There are people who can be wiser than you.

107 Wamampha abaya

The good is not spared

Expl: Often good people do not live long.

108 Warawantha nge garu yarya mwana waki

To talk like a dog which has eaten his puppies

Expl: A person who talks nonsense.

109 Wasawasawa nge nyoli yapa mazila

To be restless as a chicken which is laying eggs

Expl: A person who is restless.

110 Wendi nthende-uzi

A sickly person

Expl: A person is always weak and feeble—AIDS would be a good example.

111 Wendi twa mumatakama

A liar

Expl: A person who is a double dealer.

112 Yo wacheuka ndikuti wavwa mswayo

A person who turns aside has heard some noise

Expl: A person who feels something reacts to it.

113 Yo wachiwona ndiyu wathawa

He/she who has seen it is the one who runs away

Expl: A person who is concerned responds accordingly.

114 Yo waweja wawoneka ndi sazi paku pauka

The one who is a good fisherman returns home with some fish

Expl: A person who works hard gets good results.

115 Zina litufwa cha

A name does not die

Expl: If a good person dies, his/her name is always remembered; or, children prolong the name of the clan.

116 Zuma ndizu ateghe mani, mbulika cha

"*Zuma*" is what can be caught by using leaves and not "*mbulika*"

Expl: There are certain things you cannot hide, or, what you do in secret will be publicly known one day.

202

Appendix B: Note on the African Proverbs Project

The African Proverbs Project was created and led by an ad hoc working group including Stan Nussbaum (American, coordinator) John Mbiti (Kenyan), Joshua Kudadjie (Ghanaian), John Pobee (Ghanaian), Laurent Nare (Burkinabe), Willem Saayman (South African) and Dan Hoffman (American). The members were chosen not because of a deep specialist interest in proverbs but because they all see the significance of proverbs in their broader fields and they all have a broad range of contacts through different networks. The role of the committee was to find and encourage the proverb experts, not duplicate or compete with their work.

The African Proverbs Project was funded principally by The Pew Charitable Trusts of Philadelphia, Pennsylvania, USA, from 1993-1996. A national and international philanthropy with a special commitment to Philadelphia, The Pew Charitable Trusts support nonprofit activities in the areas of culture, education, the environment, health and human services, public policy, and religion. Through their grant-making, the Trusts seek to encourage individual development and personal achievement, cross-disciplinary problem solving, and innovative, practical approaches to meeting the changing needs of a global community.

The two organizations under whose umbrella the Project operated are both Christian mission agencies who see this Project as integrally related to their broader work. One is Joint Ministry in Africa, which combines the Africa work of two denominations, the United Church of Christ and the Christian Church (Disciples of Christ). The other is Global Mapping International, an independent evangelical mission agency with a staff of six persons who raise their own salary support from a broad spectrum of churches and individuals.

In addition to the Proverbs for Preaching and Teaching Series, the African Proverbs Project included the following elements:

A Consultation on African Proverbs and Theological Education, Ricatla Theological Seminary, Maputo, Mozambique, March 1995. Papers edited by John S. Pobee, *Proverbs and African Christianity*.

An Interdisciplinary Symposium on the African Proverb in the 21st Century, University of South Africa, Pretoria, October 1995. Papers edited by Willem Saayman, *Embracing the Baobab Tree* (Pretoria: Unisa Press, 1997).

The *African Proverbs Series*; General Editor John S. Mbiti (Pretoria: Unisa Press, 1997). 500 to 1500 proverbs in each volume with translations, explanations, illustrations and index. Proverbs are arranged in similar topical sections in each volume for easy comparison. Series Editor: Rev. Prof. Dr. John S. Mbiti. Writers commissioned by the African Proverbs Project for work on proverbs from Ghana, Uganda, Ethiopia, Lesotho and Burkina Faso.

"Endangered Proverbs" Collections. 100-300 proverbs in languages where few if any proverbs have been previously published with translations. Collectors recruited by the African Proverbs Project and paid per proverb submitted from Burkina Faso, Togo and South Africa.

Three annotated bibliographies: one on African proverb scholarship (Mieder), one on African proverb collections (Nussbaum), and one on the pastoral use of African proverbs (Healey).

Production of a CD-ROM called *The African Proverbs CD: Collections, Studies, Bibliographies* (Colorado Springs: Global Mapping International, 1996). The CD included most of the above publications plus reprints of fourteen other proverb collections and several other tools for proverb research such as:

African Languages According to the Ethnologue. A complete list of African languages with population estimates, locations, variant names, dialects, and linguistic family tree, excerpted from the Ethnologue (Dallas: SIL, 1995).

Directory of African Proverbs Researchers and Collectors. Names, addresses, publications, proverbs interests and other biographical information about people who have contributed to the collection and/or study of African proverbs.

Statistical Tables and Maps on the Status of Proverb Collecting in Each Language and Country.

Web site: www.afriprov.org

Though it was not envisioned at the time the African Proverbs Project was designed or funded from project money, a web site was created by a number of interested persons and groups in Kenya and Tanzania, carrying on activities that relate to the vision of the Project. An East African center for ongoing proverb research was also launched by Hekima College in Nairobi.